Opposing
Viewpoints®

Other Books of Related Interest in the Opposing Viewpoints Series:

Male/Female Roles
Problems of Death
Science and Religion
Sexual Values

Additional Books in the Opposing Viewpoints Series:

American Foreign Policy
The American Military
American Values
America's Prisons
The Arms Race
Censorship
Central America
Chemical Dependency
Constructing a Life Philosophy
Crime & Criminals
Criminal Justice
Death & Dying
The Death Penalty
The Ecology Controversy
The Energy Crisis
The Middle East
Nuclear War
The Political Spectrum
Religion and Human Experience
Social Justice
The Vietnam War
War and Human Nature
The Welfare State

ABORTION

Opposing Viewpoints®

David L. Bender & Bruno Leone, *Series Editors*

Bonnie Szumski, *Book Editor*

Greenhaven Press
577 Shoreview Park Road
St. Paul, Minnesota 55126

Library of Congress Cataloging-in-Publication Data

Abortion, opposing viewpoints.

(Opposing viewpoints series)
Bibliography: p.
Includes index.
Summary: Presents opposing viewpoints about various aspects of abortion, including its morality and legality. Includes critical thinking skill activities and a list of organizations to contact.
1. Abortion—United States—Addresses, essays, lectures. 2. Abortion—United States—Moral and ethical aspects—Addresses, essays, lectures. [1. Abortion—Addresses, essays, lectures] I. Szumski, Bonnie, 1958- . II. Series.
HQ767.5.U5A266 1986 363.4'6 86-302
ISBN 0-89908-380-3 (lib. bdg.)
ISBN 0-89908-355-2 (pbk.)

"Congress shall make no law . . . abridging the freedom of speech, or of the press."

First Amendment to the US Constitution

The basic foundation of our democracy is the first amendment guarantee of freedom of expression. The *Opposing Viewpoints Series* is dedicated to the concept of this basic freedom and the idea that it is more important to practice it than to enshrine it.

Contents

Why Consider Opposing Viewpoints?

"It is better to debate a question without settling it than to settle a question without debating it."

Joseph Joubert (1754-1824)

The Importance of Examining Opposing Viewpoints

The purpose of the Opposing Viewpoints books, and this book in particular, is to present balanced, and often difficult to find, opposing points of view on complex and sensitive issues.

Probably the best way to become informed is to analyze the positions of those who are regarded as experts and well studied on issues. It is important to consider every variety of opinion in an attempt to determine the truth. Opinions from the mainstream of society should be examined. But also important are opinions that are considered radical, reactionary, or minority as well as those stigmatized by some other uncomplimentary label. An important lesson of history is the eventual acceptance of many unpopular and even despised opinions. The ideas of Socrates, Jesus, and Galileo are good examples of this.

Readers will approach this book with their own opinions on the issues debated within it. However, to have a good grasp of one's own viewpoint, it is necessary to understand the arguments of those with whom one disagrees. It can be said that those who do not completely understand their adversary's point of view do not fully understand their own.

A persuasive case for considering opposing viewpoints has been presented by John Stuart Mill in his work *On Liberty*. When examining controversial issues it may be helpful to reflect on this suggestion:

> The only way in which a human being can make some approach to knowing the whole of a subject, is by hearing what can be said about it by persons of every variety of opinion, and studying all modes in which it can be looked at by every character of mind. No wise man ever acquired his wisdom in any mode but this.

Analyzing Sources of Information

The Opposing Viewpoints Series includes diverse materials taken from magazines, journals, books, and newspapers, as well as statements and position papers from a wide range of individuals, organizations and governments. This broad spectrum of sources helps to develop patterns of thinking which are open to the consideration of a variety of opinions.

Pitfalls to Avoid

A pitfall to avoid in considering opposing points of view is that of regarding one's own opinion as being common sense and the most rational stance and the point of view of others as being only opinion and naturally wrong. It may be that another's opinion is correct and one's own is in error.

Another pitfall to avoid is that of closing one's mind to the opinions of those with whom one disagrees. The best way to approach a dialogue is to make one's primary purpose that of understanding the mind and arguments of the other person and not that of enlightening him or her with one's own solutions. More can be learned by listening than speaking.

It is my hope that after reading this book the reader will have a deeper understanding of the issues debated and will appreciate the complexity of even seemingly simple issues on which good and honest people disagree. This awareness is particularly important in a democratic society such as ours where people enter into public debate to determine the common good. Those with whom one disagrees should not necessarily be regarded as enemies, but perhaps simply as people who suggest different paths to a common goal.

Developing Basic Reading and Thinking Skills

In this book, carefully edited opposing viewpoints are purposely placed back to back to create a running debate; each viewpoint is preceded by a short quotation that best expresses the author's main argument. This format instantly plunges the reader into the midst of a controversial issue and greatly aids that reader in mastering the basic skill of recognizing an author's point of view.

A number of basic skills for critical thinking are practiced in the activities that appear throughout the books in the series. Some of the skills are:

Evaluating Sources of Information The ability to choose from among alternative sources the most reliable and accurate source in relation to a given subject.

Separating Fact from Opinion The ability to make the basic distinction between factual statements (those that can be demonstrated or verified empirically) and statements of opinion (those that are beliefs or attitudes that cannot be proved).

Identifying Stereotypes The ability to identify oversimplified, exaggerated descriptions (favorable or unfavorable) about people and insulting statements about racial, religious or national groups, based upon misinformation or lack of information.

Recognizing Ethnocentrism The ability to recognize attitudes or opinions that express the view that one's own race, culture, or group is inherently superior, or those attitudes that judge another culture or group in terms of one's own.

It is important to consider opposing viewpoints and equally important to be able to critically analyze those viewpoints. The activities in this book are designed to help the reader master these thinking skills. Statements are taken from the book's viewpoints and the reader is asked to analyze them. This technique aids the reader in developing skills that not only can be applied to the viewpoints in this book, but also to situations where opinionated spokespersons comment on controversial issues. Although the activities are helpful to the solitary reader, they are most useful when the reader can benefit from the interaction of group discussion.

Using this book and others in the series should help readers develop basic reading and thinking skills. These skills should improve the reader's ability to understand what they read. Readers should be better able to separate fact from opinion, substance from rhetoric and become better consumers of information in our media-centered culture.

This volume of the Opposing Viewpoints Series does not advocate a particular point of view. Quite the contrary! The very nature of the book leaves it to the reader to formulate the opinions he or she finds most suitable. My purpose as publisher is to see that this is made possible by offering a wide range of viewpoints which are fairly presented.

David L. Bender
Publisher

Introduction

"A fetus is no more a human being than an acorn is an oak tree."

Caroline Lund and Cindy Jaquith,
Abortion: A Woman's Right, 1971.

"There is no abortion that is not the unjust taking of another's life."

James T. Burtchaell,
Rachel Weeping: The Case Against Abortion, 1982.

Few issues have fostered such contention and resulted in such polarization as has the topic of abortion. The participants in the abortion debate not only have firmly-fixed beliefs, but each group has a self-designated appellation—pro-choice and pro-life—that clearly reflects what they believe to be the essential issues. On one side, the pro-choice camp sees individual choice as central to the debate: If a woman cannot choose to terminate an unwanted pregnancy, a condition which affects her own body and possibly her entire life, then she has lost one of her most basic human rights. These proponents of abortion believe that while the fetus is a potential life, its life cannot be placed on the same level with that of the woman. On the other side, the pro-life opponents of abortion argue that the fetus is human and therefore endowed with the same human rights as the mother. Stated simply, they believe that when a society legalizes abortion, it is sanctioning murder.

Abortion is *not* a contemporary issue. Historically, both tribal and urbanized societies have employed a variety of methods to end unwanted pregnancies. Germaine Greer in her book *Sex and Destiny* described some of the abortion methods used throughout the world. They include the application of pressure outside the womb—using logs and rocks and jumping on the woman's abdomen—as well as internal methods such as the ingestion of highly toxic chemicals and the use of various implements inside the uterus. In today's more industrialized societies, technology has simplified the abortion procedure to a few basic, safe methods. However, technology has also enhanced society's knowledge of the fetus. Ultrasound, fetal therapy, and amniocentesis graphically reveal complex life before birth, and it is this potential—and many say actual—human life that is at the heart of the debate.

An editor seeking material for a book on abortion in the 1980s can find literally thousands of articles, newsletters, and books on the topic. The issue is evident in radio, television, newspaper headlines, magazines, nonfiction, and even fiction books. But the editor's selection process is complicated by the overwhelming sensitivity the issue generates for people. Deep-seated views on both sides make the task of compiling an unbiased book on abortion a complicated and touchy one.

The editors of *Abortion: Opposing Viewpoints* have attempted to collect the most representative arguments on the abortion debate. They have endeavored to include prominent pro-life and pro-choice publications and authors who write from conviction, and in many cases, personal experience. Also included are the positions of organizations, with one notable exception, Planned Parenthood, which refused permission to reprint some of its materials. Perhaps the refusal of this prominent pro-choice organization is testimony to the sensitivity of the issue.

These difficulties could have prompted Greenhaven Press to abandon the topic. However, the issue of abortion, perhaps more so than most others today, finds few advocates taking the proverbial "middle ground." It is this polarity that makes abortion particularly suited to the opposing viewpoints approach. The six key topics debated are: When Does Life Begin? Should Abortion Remain a Personal Choice? Is Abortion Immoral? Can Abortion Be Justified? Should Abortion Remain Legal? Are Extremist Tactics Justified in the Abortion Debate? As the reader examines the highly charged viewpoints in this book, he or she will be faced with many thought-provoking and perhaps unsolvable questions about the nature of life. One matter seems certain: As long as contraceptives are not completely reliable and safe, or men and women neglect their use, abortion will remain an issue.

CHAPTER 1

When Does Life Begin?

VIEWPOINT 1

"I accept what is biologically manifest—that human life commences at the time of conception."

Human Life Begins at Conception

Landrum B. Shettles and David Rorvik

Landrum B. Shettles holds Ph.D. and M.D. degrees from Johns Hopkins University. For twenty-seven years he was the attending obstetrician-gynecologist at Columbia-Presbyterian Medical Center in New York City. He has specialized in research in fertility, sterility, and diseases of newborn infants. He first discovered and distinguished between male and female producing sperm, and he continues to pioneer research in in vitro fertilization. David Rorvik is a former science and medical reporter for *Time.* He also won a Pulitzer Traveling Fellowship. In the following viewpoint, the authors argue that there is one fact that no one can deny: the life of biological human beings begins at conception.

As you read, consider the following questions:

1. Why do the authors reject the idea that the fetus is only a potential life?
2. Why do the authors believe that the unborn is "always a distinct human being"?
3. Why do the authors oppose abortion?

Most of the billions of cells that collectively make up a human being are "soma" (Greek for "body") cells. Unless manipulated in exotic ways, these body cells are and remain just what they appear to be: skin, hair, bone, muscle, and so on. Each has some worthy, special function in life, a function that it dutifully, if narrowly, performs until it dies. And the soma cells *do* die, ultimately leaving nothing of themselves behind.

There are some other, far rarer cells, however,—known as "germ" cells or "sex" cells—that have the power not only to extravagantly transform themselves, giving rise to *every* other kind of human cell, but also to seize for themselves a bit of the "impossible": immortality. The sex cells are the sperm cells in the male and the egg cells in the female. It is only in combination, one with the other, that these cells can work their special magic, rise above the humdrum stasis of their somatic siblings, and confer something of their essences upon the future generations in which they will thus perpetuate themselves.

There is an "essense" in every cell, whether somatic or germinal, consisting of the nucleic acids, principally deoxyribonucleic acid—better known as "DNA," the basic stuff that forms the "building blocks" of life, the genes and chromosomes. Actually the genes are made up of much smaller units, so numerous that if you were by some miracle able to completely "unravel" the strands of DNA that exist in a single human being the "chain of life" would stretch across some millions of miles. There are many thousands of genes in the nucleus (central core) of each cell; these are arranged in larger chromosomal units, of which there are forty-six in each human body cell. The individual sex cells, sperm and egg, on the other hand, contain only half that number: twenty-three chromosomes each. It is only through combination, through merger, that the sex cells attain the full complement of hereditary units that defines a human being. . . .

The Merging of Egg and Sperm

The merger [of egg and sperm] is complete within twelve hours, at which time the egg—which may have "waited" as many as forty years for this moment—is fertilized and becomes known technically as the "zygote," containing the full set of forty-six chromosomes required to create new human life. Conception has occurred. The genotype—the inherited characteristics of a unique human being—is established in the conception process and will remain in force for the entire life of that individual. No other event in biological life is so decisive as this one; no other set of circumstances can even remotely rival genotype in "making you what you are."

Conception confers life and makes that life one of a kind. Unless you have an identical twin, there is virtually no chance, in the natural course of things, that there will ever be "another you"—

not even if mankind were to persist for billions of years. Indeed, given the vast number of combinations possible among chromosomes, genes, and their smaller subparts, there is virtually no chance that even your own parents could ever come up with another "copy" of you, not even if by some magic they could produce millions of offspring. . . .

Many who have studied the data regarding twins have declared themselves awed and astounded by the evident, sometimes overwhelming power of heredity. Even twins who have grown up in radically different home environments have exhibited, upon observation in later life, astonishing behavioral similarities. A significant number are found to have adopted remarkably similar lifestyles, often choosing the same occupations, marrying women who are alike in too many particulars to be accounted for by coincidence alone, and so on. The genotype that is conferred at conception does not merely start life, it *defines* life.

When Does Human Life Begin?

Scientists identify the first moment of human life as that instant when a sperm cell unites with an ovum or egg cell. Prior to this moment, the ovum was inching its way toward and through the womb in just the same manner as do the hundreds of ova that are produced during a woman's reproductive years. At the moment of fertilization, however, this ovum takes on an entirely different destiny. The sperm penetrates the ovum and 15,000 genes from the nucleus of the sperm and 15,000 from the nucleus of the ovum form a unique combination that is nothing less than a new human being at the earliest stages of his or her life.

Catherine and William Odell, *Visitor,* January 16, 1983.

Conception sets in motion a series of events within the womb more complex and wonderous than anything that will ever happen to the body outside the womb. So astonishing are the happenings that transpire in the first moments, days, weeks, and months of life-before-birth that when we come to understand them fully we will very likely possess the answer to such puzzles as cancer and the aging process. By fully understanding life we will almost certainly be able to better understand death. . . .

Is There Life Before Conception?

Fascinating and purposeful though the sex cells are, ova and spermatozoa do *not* by themselves constitute human life. The sex cells are "half worlds" which only become whole in combination with each other—through the process I have described. This process helps to ensure, through its nearly infinite recombinant genetic possibilities, the continued variability, adaptability, and development of the species. In returning to the opening question, it may seem that I am belaboring the obvious; but the question does have some bearing on the abortion debate.

Some pro-abortionists of the "life-is-a-continuum" school of thought have attempted to belittle the significance of the human zygote (fertilized egg), claiming it is no more worthy to be considered human life than is a single egg or sperm cell. Indeed, some go so far as to claim that if you can call the zygote human life, then you can call every other cell in the body human life as well. . . .

There may be some arguing in this fashion who earnestly believe that they have perceived a chink in the anti-abortion position, but most, I am convinced, are being disingenuous. . . .

There is another argument sometimes raised by the pro-abortionists that should be dealt with here. The fact that a significant number of zygotes fail to implant and therefore do not result in pregnancy is seized upon by a few as "evidence" that "even Mother Nature" does not consider the fertilized egg genuine human life, any more than "she" does the hundreds of thousands of eggs and millions of sperm that are "wasted." To this I can only answer that there are also a significant number of one-year-old infants who will never make it to old age, to puberty, or even to their second birthday. . . . Does the fact that life is interrupted at some point after it has begun mean that it never existed? . . .

A Distinct Entity

It should be understood that though I use different terms to describe the unborn—*zygote, embryo, fetus*—these labels do not reflect distinctly different phases of development; these terms are used as a matter of convenience to describe general changes. Some describe the "zygote" as becoming the "embryo" at the time of implantation; others say the "embryo stage" begins in the third week of pregnancy. Some say the "fetal stage" begins in the fifth week of development; others say the eighth week, and still others say the embryo does not become the fetus until the end of the first trimester. It is my view that once the major processes of differentiation are largely complete, the embryo becomes the fetus. That occurs by the end of the eighth week.

Whatever the terminology, the unborn is *always* a distinct entity, an individual human life in its own right and not simply some "disposable part of the mother's body," as some pro-abortionists argue. Fetologist Albert W. Liley has asserted: "It is the fetus who is in charge of the pregnancy." Even some who oppose restrictions on abortion would readily agree. For example, Daniel Callahan, director of the Institute of Society, Ethics and the Life Sciences, has stated: "Genetically, hormonally and in all organic respects save for the source of its nourishment, a fetus and even an embryo is separate from the woman." . . .

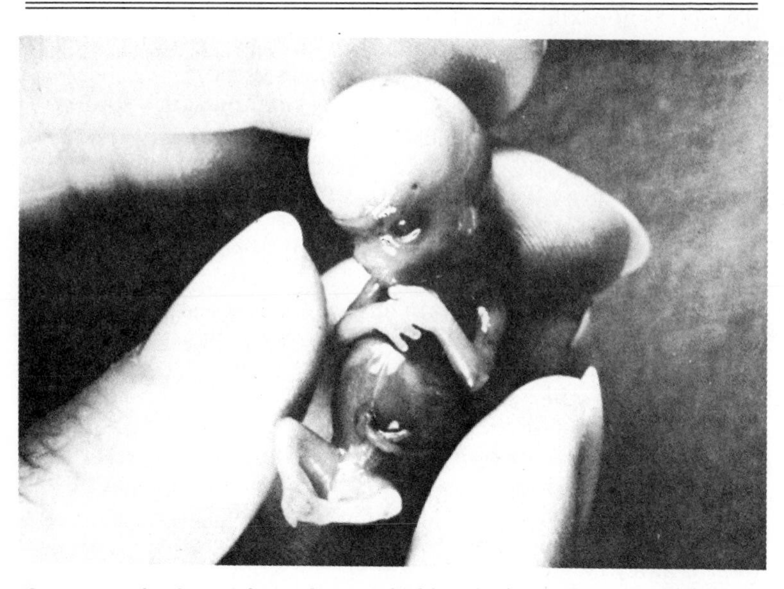

Spontaneously aborted fetus photographed by Charles O. Garrison, M.D.

I cringe whenever I hear someone utter the phrase, "It's just a blob," which the pro-abortionists frequently use to refer to the fetus in the first and even the second trimesters of development. Even some pro-abortion scientists refer to the fetus, at this and later stages, as "a mass of cells" or "mere tissue," in efforts to justify not only the abortion, but even also experimentation on the unborn. Some who employ this terminology are genuinely ignorant of the facts; some others, I suspect are willing to overlook the biological facts, convinced that abortion is an acceptable means to a desired end. . . .

My Position

I oppose abortion. I do so, first, because I accept what is biologically manifest—that human life commences at the time of conception—and, second, because I believe it is wrong to take innocent human life under any circumstances. My position is scientific, pragmatic, and humanitarian. My definition of man. . . is purely biological. Biological man is the product of the forty-six chromosomes that combine to confer a unique identity at the time an egg is fertilized by a sperm. I am not qualified to address issues of soul and spirit in any detail. It is my assumption, based entirely on faith, not science, that to the extent that biological man is imbued with a soul, he acquires that property at the moment of conception.

I reject all the arguments which seek to justify abortion on grounds that the unborn is not a living being or is somehow less than human, mere "potential life," or part of a "continuum of life that has neither beginning nor end." I resist and reject the new ethic which—even when it recognizes that the unborn child is not only human life, but meaningful human life—still considers that life expendable under many circumstances. The pragmatism that this ethic purports to embrace is, in my view, illusory; an ethic that makes any class of individuals expendable "in the interests of society" ultimately imperils that entire society.

I have always opposed abortion, except in those cases where the life of the woman is genuinely endangered by a continuation of the pregnancy. For some time, however, my position was one of "passive resistance." It was not until the 1973 Supreme Court decision that I made a public statement opposed to abortion. . . .

It comes as a surprise to some of my associates that I oppose abortion, particularly since I pioneered some of the technology that made the so-called test-tube babies a reality. Because some of those who have opposed abortion have also opposed the creation of human life in the laboratory, the assumption has often been made that I would automatically be *pro-abortion*. Thus, I've learned a good deal about stereotyping. Now that I've made my anti-abortion views known, some seem to think that, "in order to be consistent," I will also become Catholic, vote for "hard-line conservatives," oppose civil rights, birth control, and education, and adopt some anti-feminist views. At the very least some seem to expect me to account for my new outspokenness by declaring that I "saw the light" as a result of a mystical religious experience. After all, I am told, "Everyone knows that abortion is a religious issue."

Being Anti-Abortion

In truth, there are some—a very few, in my experience—on the pro-abortion side who would like to see me embrace this stereotype. But I refuse to become wedded to either a conservative or a liberal political and ideological stereotype.

Far from being inconsistent with "liberal" or "humanist" principles, I believe that abhorrence for abortion squares precisely with those values. I believe that the clearest-headed pragmatists and "situational ethicists" *must* oppose abortion if they truly do prize the "greatest good for the greatest number." The Golden Rule is pragmatism of the highest order.

As for my position on abortion in my own medical practice, I try not to preach or proselytize. If a couple comes to me seeking an abortion or advice on abortion, I am pleased to be able to present my viewpoint. But for the most part, my approach is to show rather than to tell. I show the woman or the couple pictures of the unborn at various stages of development, explain what we know about the fetus at critical stages, and then let the parent or parents make up their own minds. If presenting the facts in an objective manner makes me guilty of attempting to "bias" the decision, then I stand guilty as charged.

We do well to remember that behind the barrage of words that make up the raging debate, there are real people, real feelings, real hopes, fears, triumphs, and tragedies.

VIEWPOINT 2

"*The possession of forty-six chromosomes does not make a cell a person.*"

Human Life Does Not Begin at Conception

Frank R. Zindler

Formerly a professor of biology and geology, Frank R. Zindler is now a science writer. A member of the American Association for the Advancement of Science, the American Chemical Society, and the American Schools of Oriental Research, he is also co-chairperson of the Committee of Correspondence on Evolution Education and Director of the Central Ohio Chapter of American Atheists. In the following viewpoint, Mr. Zindler argues that in order to be a human, a fetus must have a personality. Since it obviously lacks a personality, its rights should in no way supersede those of a pregnant woman.

As you read, consider the following questions:

1. What is the author's view of abortion as a contraceptive?
2. How many conceptions end in spontaneous abortion, according to the author? How does this support the author's argument that a fetus is not a human?
3. How would illegal abortion "subordinate the rights of actual persons to the imagined rights of eggs," according to the author?

Frank R. Zindler, "An Acorn Is Not an Oak Tree," *American Atheist*, August 1985. Reprinted with the author's permission.

When the Supreme Court of the United States of America decided on January 22, 1973, that women have a right to control their own reproductive destinies, it struck down the state laws which had made early abortions illegal. This allowed women to take a great step forward in their quest for social equality with men. Unfortunately, the Court was not as well-informed on the scientific and philosophical issues as it might have been, and although it came to what I consider to be the right conclusions, it did so partly for the wrong reasons.

While the Supreme Court did recognize the importance of the question "Is the fetus a person?" it was unable to break away from the irrelevant question "When does life begin?" Consequently, the court's deliberations were hampered by an incorrect formulation of the central question at issue. Clearly, the question does not concern the beginning of "life." The unfertilized egg is alive, the sperm is alive, and no one has ever suggested that live babies result from dead sperm or eggs. Human life is part of a living continuum stretching back to the dawning days of the planet.

Despite the shaky scientific foundations of its decision, the Court made a statement of great practical utility. It declared, in effect, that during the first trimester of pregnancy, when abortion is far safer for a woman than is childbirth, essentially no restrictions can be placed upon a woman's right to privacy and upon her right to refuse to provide room and board for an uninvited guest. During the second trimester also, a woman's rights overshadow the "rights" of the fetus. During this period, the state may regulate abortion, but only to provide for the well-being of the woman—not because of fetal "rights."

Only during the third trimester, when the fetus becomes "viable"—capable of surviving on its own outside the mother's body—does the state begin to have a legitimate interest in the "rights" of the unborn. Even so, the mother's health is judged to be of greater importance than the life of the fetus. . . .

Compulsory Pregnancy

Isn't abortion more a social problem than a religious problem?

Of course, abortion—like all aspects of human reproductive behavior and personal freedom—is a "social" problem. If the Roman Catholic Church and several of the more strident fundamentalist Protestant churches were not, however, trying to force their religious dogmas on society by force of law and constitutional amendment, women would find less opposition to their quest for self-determination in the area of reproductive rights. Opposing freedom of choice in the matter of abortion is tantamount to advocating compulsory pregnancy after rape, incest, or contraceptive failure. In the matter of abortion, as with all "pelvic issues," most of the shackles which restrain human freedom have been imposed by religious groups, directly or indirectly. . . .

But doesn't the fetus move, show sensitivity to pain, and have a heartbeat and brain waves?

All this is true, but this does not make the fetus a person. To be a person, there must be evidence of a personality. Dogs, frogs, and earthworms have all the characteristics listed, but that is insufficient to make them persons.

Fetuses and Infants Different

A fertilized egg has become implanted in the uterus at the end of two weeks. At this point, the product of conception begins to receive nourishment from the mother and is called an embryo. Six weeks later the various organ systems are well-defined, and the embryo progresses to the stage of a fetus. For the first 24 weeks of pregnancy, the fetus is completely dependent on maternal nutritional support and is nonviable if separated from the mother through a miscarriage or accident. Nowhere in the world would such a fetus be listed in the vital statistics as a stillborn infant.

Alex Gerber, *Los Angeles Times*, May 26, 1985.

A brief review of human embryology is in order. It takes more than ten days after fertilization for the conceptus to become anything more than a hollow ball of cells at the stage of development of certain colonial algae. During the first week, it is free-floating and not even attached to the uterine wall. Not until the beginning of the fourth week does a heart begin to beat, and then it is two-chambered like that of a fish. Not until the end of the fifth week is there evidence of the beginning of formation of the cerebral hemispheres, and they are merely hollow bubbles of cells. Hemisphere development reaches reptile-grade during the fourth month, and primitive mammal-grade (opossum) during the sixth month.

Human Fetus at Five Weeks

Figure 1 shows the human fetus after five weeks of development. A prominent yolk-sac is visible, as if the embryo were that of a reptile developing within a yolk-containing egg. The heart is two-chambered like that of a fish, and in the neck region we see prominent gill-clefts. The arteries carrying blood from the heart to the gills recapitulate in minute detail the aortic-arch structures of fishes. Like the embryonic gills of fishes, the embryonic gills of humans lack the feathery respiratory tissues characteristic of mature gills.

This alleged person has two tiny, hollow bubbles of tissue for cerebral hemispheres, and it has mesonephric kidneys such as are

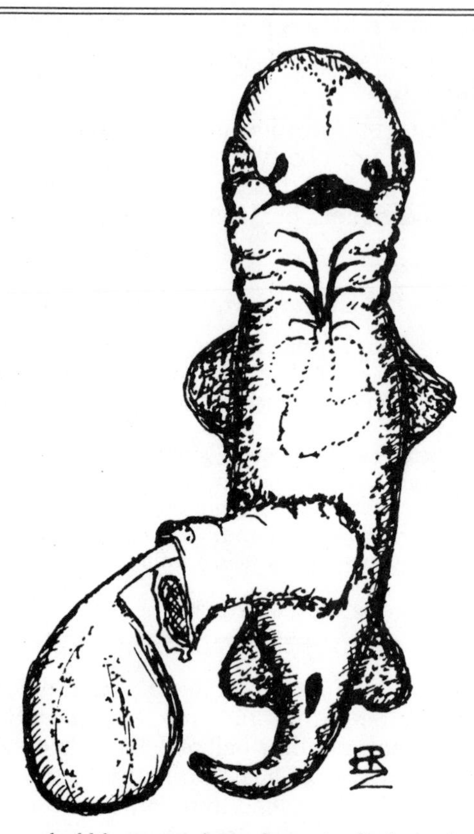

Figure 1. A five-week-old human embryo, drawn to eliminate the natural curvatures and to increase visibility of fish-like features. Easily seen are the gill-clefts, the two-chambered heart, the tail, the unpartitioned cloaca (anal opening), and the prominent yolk-sac (a reptilian feature).

found in fishes and amphibians. In fact, it still has traces of pronephric kidneys, the type found in the most primitive vertebrate known to science, the hermaphroditic hagfish!

Sexually, the embryo is indeterminate, still possessing an all-purpose anal opening, the cloaca. Although later in development this structure will become partitioned (into two separate openings in males, three in females), at this stage it is just like that of fishes. Just posterior to the cloaca is a tail which resembles the tail of a salamander. . . .

I agree that if the mother's life is endangered by pregnancy she should be allowed an abortion if it is needed to save her life. But I don't believe abortion should be a substitute for birth control.

We agree that abortion is a less desirable option as compared with contraception. But contraception often fails, and the same church which opposes abortion also opposes sterilization and contraception—thus creating a greater need for abortion than otherwise would exist. If one admits abortion to save a woman's life, one is admitting that the fetus is less important than the woman who incubates it. Once one has admitted this, one no longer has any grounds to accord full, legal personhood upon the fetus or . . . upon the fertilized egg itself.

Women and Zygotes

All right, I changed my mind. Abortion should not *be allowed to save a woman's life. I think the soul* does *enter the zygote at the moment of conception.*

If the single-celled zygote is *equal* to a full-grown woman, it follows that a full-grown woman can't be worth *more* than a single cell! Any one who values women so little is a menace to society and shouldn't be allowed to run loose without a leash. . . .

But the zygote has forty-six human chromosomes and is a unique genetic being. It is at least a potential human being and should be protected as something very valuable.

The possession of forty-six chromosomes does not make a cell a person. Most of the cells of your body contain these forty-six chromosomes, but that does not make a white corpuscle a person! As for the significance of uniqueness, identical quintuplets are genetically identical, yet they have personal identities apart from their genetic endowment. The development of cloning will make the cellular offspring from a single zygote—all the cells being genetically identical—into a veritable army of genetically identical but different persons. Moreover, not every zygote contains forty-six chromosomes. Zygotes destined to develop into mentally retarded individuals with Down's Syndrome ("Mongolism") have forty-seven chromosomes, and a variety of other developmental defects are know which involve possession of fewer than forty-six chromosomes. Quite literally, such individuals are born without all their pieces! If possession of forty-six chromosomes make some thing a person, then it would seem that possession of a different number would make something else.

All Cells Are Human

As for potential human beings, *an acorn is not an oak tree!* With cloning, every nucleated cell in your body is a potential person. This being the case, brushing one's teeth should be a crime on a par with murder since one destroys countless epithelial "potential people" with every scrape across the gums. *Fully one-third of all conceptions end in spontaneous abortion,* often at very early stages of development. Is god to blame for this? Should he/she/it be blamed for the destruction of so many "potential people"? And what of the case where the conceptus develops into a creature lacking a cerebral cortex? . . .

Religion and Women's Humanity

The opponents of freedom of choice generally are the same people who believe in the biblical notion that women are second-class creatures. They belong to churches which suppress women on the grounds that they are god's afterthought—a spare rib grown into a temptress who brought destruction into the Garden of Eden. . . .

An Atheist woman is a complete person in her own right. She works with men as an equal. She has a right to decide how and when to employ *all* the organ systems of her own body. She is worth more than a fetus and infinitely more than a zygote! No pope or preacher or president has the moral right to tell her that she must submit to the doctrine of "obedience." No one has the right to deny to her the self-determination granted automatically to men. Let no one ever again subordinate the rights of actual persons—women—to the imagined rights of eggs!

VIEWPOINT 3

"Every time the unborn child becomes the beneficiary of treatment formerly reserved for those after birth, a spotlight . . . is focused on the inherent humanity of life in the womb."

Advancing Medical Technology Proves Fetal Viability

William Brennan

In the last decade remarkable advances have been made in fetal medicine. Corrective surgery on the fetus for congenital deformities and diseases has been making headline news. This remarkable technology has generated a new controversy over the issue of the right to abortion. Many wonder if medical technology has been responsible for lowering the fetal age at which an abortion should be allowed. In the following viewpoint, William Brennan, a professor of social services at St. Louis University, bases his case against abortion on these medical advances.

As you read, consider the following questions:

1. The author argues that ultrasound and fetology have increased public knowledge about life in the womb. What other benefits does ultrasound offer?
2. Why does the author believe that abortion should be eliminated?

William Brennan, "Abortion Technology and Fetal Therapy: On a Collision Course." Reprinted from TO RESCUE THE FUTURE with permission of Life Cycle Books, PO Box 792, Lewiston, NY 14092-0792 (416) 690-5860.

Contrary to pro-abortion mythology, the greatest threat to today's abortion-industrial complex does not come from heavy-handed tactics of the so-called radical right or the imposition of sectarian morality by alleged religious zealots, but from fetologists and surgeons pioneering radical new methods of treating unborn children.

The life-enhancing thrust of fetal surgery stands in stark opposition to the life-denying emphasis of abortion technology. Each advance in fetal therapy will crystallize the inherent contradiction between the therapeutic medicine of fetologists and the exterminative medicine of the abortionists. To understand why fetology is threatening the very foundation of abortion, it is important to understand the "genius" of mass destruction. . . .

Modern Medicine Against Itself

The womb as a surgical theater for the unborn is the perfect paradigm for the schizophrenic world of contemporary medicine where killing and curing share a perverse state of professional compatibility. Developments in fetal therapy will, however, make it increasingly difficult to ignore, let alone tolerate, the deplorable condition of modern medical ethics in which too many physicians have regressed back to the dark age of pre-Hippocratic medicine where they once again function in the schizophrenic role of killer-healer.

The miracle technologies of ultrasound, fetoscopy, and hysteroscopy have opened up unprecedented windows on the womb. They reveal compellingly that the tiny passenger within is nothing less than a bona fide human being from the very onset of pregnancy, and they make the surgical treatment of that unborn human being increasingly routine. Planned Parenthood executive Alfred Moran warned his cohorts at a National Abortion Federation meeting in 1982 that "we are going to find ourselves isolated" unless "we are prepared to begin to recognize that technology and medical sciences and perceptions of fetal viability are radically changing in our society." He was particularly horrified by the potential that the new life-promoting fetal therapy has for jeopardizing the right to abortion: "We begin to see the fetus as a patient; which tends to personalize it," he observed.

A Spotlight on the Womb

Every time the unborn child becomes the beneficiary of treatment formerly reserved for those after birth, a spotlight of increasing intensity is focused on the inherent humanity of life in the womb. The implementation of abortion technology—built on a depersonalized, anachronistic perception of unwanted unborn children as pregnancy tissue or subhuman entities—is running on a direct collision course with the science of fetology, which is forging powerful, personalized images of the fetus as a legitimate patient deserving the best care and treatment possible. The consequences of this strongly emerging perception are far-reaching. It is but a short step from the image of the fetus as a legitimate patient to a view of the fetus as a legal person with constitutional rights.

A New Phase of the Human Life Cycle

Progress in fetal surgery contains the seeds of even more profound revolutionary and long-term outcomes than saving human lives in the womb and personalizing the unborn. In the *New England Journal of Medicine* (February 17, 1983) Drs. Mark I. Evans and John C. Fletcher report on the cases of two pregnant women (one in the late first trimester and the other in the early second trimester) who decided against abortion after seeing ultrasonic pictures of their unborn children. The authors indicate that such an experience precipitated the onset of maternal bonding—the propensity of the mother to form a close emotional attachment with her baby.

Advocates for the Unborn

Advances in technology not only create new specialties, new techniques, and new ethical questions but they also create new constituencies. When fetal medicine becomes a full-fledged field of medical endeavor with specialists and even sub-specialists within it, those physicians themselves will become the loudest, most aggressive advocates for the unborn. They will be vying for Federal funds, for the positions within the universities, for their place in the medical pecking order—all in the name of their client, the human unborn.

Bernard N. Nathanson, *The Abortion Papers*, 1983.

Such evidence of intrauterine bonding during the early stages of pregnancy may well represent, according to Evans and Fletcher, part of a vast evolutionary process which will result in the establishment of a new stage of human existence—"prenatality"—a phenomenon as momentous as the many centuries of cultural and biological evolution leading to the recognition of childhood as a differentiated stage of the human life cycle. Dr. A.W. Liley's brilliant portrayal of the fetus as a personality in *Australia and New Zealand Journal of Psychiatry* in 1972 was a major forerunner of this development. His characterization of the unborn as a splendidly functioning baby rather than a poorly functioning adult provided much of the attitudinal and empirical legacy responsible for the dramatic increase in today's therapeutic efforts on behalf of the unborn now viewed as a human being existing at a legitimate phase of the human life continuum.

Through the creation of such semantic distortions as "products of conception" and "only the potentiality of life," pro-abortionists have been alarmingly effective in blocking recognition of intrauterine life as a legitimate stage in the human life cycle. To confer a status on prenatal development comparable to childhood, adolescence, and adulthood strikes at the very foundation of pro-abortion rhetoric. Such recognition would deal the anti-life forces a devastating blow.

Rationalizing the Killing

Pro-abortionists are building a set of powerful justifications for the continuation and expansion of abortion technology even in an era when the saving of unborn children will become a dominant activity of many doctors. It behooves members of the pro-life movement to get a handle on these rationalizations for killing the unborn and learn how best to counteract them. Reading the annals of Nazi medicine offers a promising approach for challenging the pro-abortion arguments, which are strikingly similar.

Although the spectacular advances in fetal therapy may force more of those in the pro-abortion camp to acknowledge the destructive nature of abortion technology, it is unlikely that they will relinquish their commitment to destroying the unwanted unborn in the most efficient manner possible. All indicators point to the increased promotion of abortion as a noble endeavor containing many indispensable benefits. This strategy will be particularly intensified in two areas: prenatal diagnosis for the detection of defects, and fetal experimentation.

Amniocentesis in conjunction with ultrasound expand the capacity to identify a growing number of abnormalities and handicaps before birth. These techniques of identification are being hailed as making significant contributions to the prevention of birth defects because those identified as defective in the womb can then be aborted. This has the effect of elevating destruction of the "unfit" to the highest level of altruism.

A blatant instance of sophisticated technology in the service of killing-redefined-as-benevolence was reported on at a press conference in June 1981. Drs. Thomas Kerenyi and Usha Chitkara of Mount Sinai Medical School in New York City announced they had killed an unwanted unborn twin with Down's syndrome by piercing his heart with a needle and extracting half his blood. Amniocentesis diagnosed Down's syndrome in one of the twins, and ultrasound enabled these medical executioners to "hit a moving target [the afflicted twin's heart] less than an inch across." This phrase surely smacks of a precision-type military operation directed against an enemy! This act of scientific barbarism was characterized by those who perpetrated it as "a very gratifying experience" on two counts: the elimination of an unwanted unfit twin and the saving of a wanted normal twin. . . .

"Such a shame. We finally score a success with a test-tube baby and now you're demanding an abortion."

Killing and healing are running on a technological collision course. They must not be allowed to co-exist; one is the very antithesis of the other. The survival of a truly civilized society where all human beings are respected and protected by law demands that abortion technology be thoroughly repudiated and recognized for what it truly is: an atavistic barbarity. . . .

The sole role of technology, especially medical technology, should be to cure, care for, and heal human lives whatever their status, condition, or stage of development. Unless this sanctity-of-life ethic is established as the prevailing norm, destructive technology run amuk will continue to engulf in its wake an ever-expanding universe of unwanted expendables before and after birth.

VIEWPOINT 4

"For the vast majority of women who have abortions, the issue of viability does not exist."

Fetal Viability Should Not Dictate Abortion Rights

Kathy Spillar

Kathy Spillar is president of the Los Angeles Chapter of the National Organization for Women. In the following viewpoint, Ms. Spillar argues that advances in medical technology have done little to change the abortion debate. Most abortions, Ms. Spillar argues, are performed long before medical advances would have an impact. Philosophical arguments over viability, while interesting, do not change the fundamental problem: women's need to decide for themselves when to terminate a pregnancy.

As you read, consider the following questions:

1. What percentage of abortions are performed by the twelfth week of pregnancy? How does this affect the viability debate, according to the author?
2. Why does the author argue most second trimester abortions are performed?
3. Why does the author believe that viability is a meaningless issue?

Kathy Spillar, "Back to Basics on Abortion: People Vs. the Unkown," *Los Angeles Times*, April 6, 1985. Reprinted with the author's permission.

"How many angels can dance on the head of a pin?" This question is at the center of the current abortion debate. At issue is whether the 1973 Roe vs. Wade Supreme Court decision is still "valid" and "workable" in an age of advancing medical technology that has become more sophisticated in sustaining premature infants.

In a brief filed by the Reagan Justice Department in two cases. . .involving a state's right to regulate abortion, this question of the "dancing angels" is examined in great detail. The Justice Department concludes that Roe vs. Wade is "flawed and arbitrary" and should be overturned as "inherently unworkable."

The reasoning goes something like this: When the Supreme Court decided Roe vs. Wade, viability—the ability of a fetus to survive outside the womb—was generally believed to be around 28 weeks of pregnancy. Now, medical advances have pushed the threshold for viability back to around 24 weeks, and some "experts" predict viability at 22 weeks in the foreseeable future. Thus the argument concludes that the medical and technical time line on which Roe vs. Wade was based is shifting. Because of this "arbitrary legal framework," Roe vs. Wade should be struck down, and states should be free to regulate abortion, deciding how far they will go in protecting a potentially viable fetus.

How Far Back?

The Justice Department and others who participate in the debate must decide the question of the "dancing angels": When is a fetus viable and when is "potential" viability an issue? Is it 24 weeks, 22 weeks, 21 weeks, 5 days? How far back do you go in recognizing any potential for viability?

This is a fascinating debate. But for the vast majority of women who have abortions, the issue of viability does not exist. Nearly 80% of abortions occur within the first 10 weeks of pregnancy. By the 12th week of pregnancy, 90% of all abortions have already been performed.

Generally, second-trimester abortions are performed only to save the woman's life or because amniocentesis (the results of which are not available until the 18th to 20th week, and in some unusual instances not until the 24th week) has revealed that the fetus has significant defects that, in the parents' judgment, are too severe to continue the pregnancy. The only other group that seeks second-trimester abortions with any frequency is teen-agers. They either don't know that they are pregnant, or are too afraid to tell a parent or other adult until they can no longer hide the pregnancy.

One Percent of Abortions Involved

In fact, viability is an issue in less than 1% of all abortions. So why is so much of the current abortion debate framed around this issue? Looking closer at who perpetuates the debate offers some insight.

It is only the most strident opponents of legal abortion who continue to argue issues such as viability. Their objective is to redirect all discussion on abortion away from the women making these choices and the reasons for their decisions, instead focusing all the debate on the fetus. They talk *only* about late-term abortions because that is the *only* argument for which they enjoy any public support.

Their strategy is to gain a wedge in the law from which to further restrict abortions. Their goal is absolute prohibition. They would permit abortion under *no* circumstances. It matters nothing to them whether viability is a factor. It matters nothing to them why women seek abortions.

Quality of Life

What is at issue for women who have abortions is the quality of their lives. They are deciding how many children they will have, and how quickly after one child they will have another. They consider the financial support that they can provide. They weigh the risks to their health and life. In the case of teen-agers, they decide to give themselves a chance to grow up.

These are meaningless issues to those who would have the Supreme Court overturn Roe vs. Wade. For now, they argue about viability. But if the current attempts to strike down the Roe decision succeed, we may no longer have to debate this question, since states will again be free to restrict abortions long before the current medically accepted point of viability.

Instead, we will begin debating a whole new question of the number of "dancing angels." We will then have to answer the question of when life begins. Is it when the fetus become viable? Shortly before the fetus becomes viable? Is it at the time the fertilized egg implants in the uterine lining? Or, is it before implantation but after fertilization? Or is it the exact moment of fertilization? Just when in this sequence of event is it all right to prevent (interrupt) a pregnancy? Just when is it abortion and when is it birth control? Does life begin with the *un*fertilized egg? How far back do you go before it's abortion?

5 VIEWPOINT

"Ultrasound . . . enables physicians to witness with the naked eye the death agonies of the infants whose lives are being ended by the healers' tools."

'The Silent Scream' Proves the Fetus Is Human

Jim Edwards

In 1984, a highly controversial film entitled *The Silent Scream* was released. Ronald Reagan showed it at the White House, and thousands of people watched it in schools, churches, and meeting halls. The film purports to be a live-action ultrasound of an ongoing abortion. In the following viewpoint, Jim Edwards, an editor of the editorial page of the *Enterprise*, a Massachusetts newspaper, believes the film once and for all solves the debate over abortion. He believes the film clearly depicts a frightened, tiny, human being struggling to escape the abortionist's persistent tools.

As you read, consider the following questions:

1. How has the media influenced the public's attitude toward abortion, according to the author?
2. What contradiction does the author see between liberals' values and their stand on abortion?

Jim Edwards, "Ultrasound Videotape Shows Unborn Infant in Death Throes," *The Union Leader*, November 20, 1984. Reprinted with permission.

"From then on there is the stalking of the victim and the victim's terror, followed by the actual dismembering of the child before your very eyes. . .you can see the spinal column. . .and the (decapitated) head is left with a piece of spine on it."

The above passage—which might have been lifted verbatim from the studio synopsis of some horror movie—is actually part of a statement made recently by Dr. Bernard Nathanson, who, as co-founder of the National Abortion Rights Action League (NARAL), presided over more than 60,000 abortions.

Dr. Nathanson stopped performing abortions after becoming aware of the sort of horrors that he describes so graphically in his new role as the pro-life movement's most distinguished convert.

For obvious reasons, The National Right to Life Committee regards Dr. Nathanson's conversion as something of a coup. His credentials are, after all, impeccable.

Dr. Nathanson owes his conversion in part to the wonders of ultrasound, which enables physicians to witness with the naked eye the death agonies of the infants whose lives are being ended by the healers' tools.

The killer of the infant whose death is described in the opening of this column served his internship under Dr. Nathanson's guidance, and the two physicians went on to become firm friends and colleagues. After Dr. Nathanson's conversion, his colleague continued to perform abortions, until witnessing the ultrasound film. One viewing of the footage was enough. Like the ultrasound technician, the doctor who had performed the abortion became so nauseated by what he had witnessed on the screen that he was forced to turn away in order to compose himself. He has never performed another abortion.

Dr. Nathanson plans to use the abortion footage as part of the presentation he makes while touring the country as a pro-life advocate. He rightly feels that the film would have a devastating impact on public opinion if he could reach a sufficient number of people.

"I think the general public is uneasy about abortion," he says, "but largely uneducated. They will take the film very seriously."

The Film Is Powerful

Indeed they will. But the film is so powerful that it also has the potential to affect the thinking of even strongly partisan audiences, and therein lies the danger it poses to the so-called pro-choice movement. Abortion advocates, most of whom belong to the generally well-educated liberal set, actually know very little about abortion. To such people, the pro-choice stance is just another piece of liberal baggage they tote around to signify their enlightenment. If you support a woman's right to control her own body, the chances are very good that you are also passionately opposed to the arms race, aid to El Salvador, school prayer, capital punishment, blood sports, the killing of whales and the clubbing to death of baby seals on the Canadian ice floes.

Liberals who pride themselves in their essential humanity work themselves up into a great state of agitation after viewing the annual seal slaughter, brought to them in living color by the networks. It is all there for them to see. The terrified flight of the cute little creatures. The thudding noise as they are brained. The death throes. The blood on the ice. It is a ghastly sight and one that leaves a lasting impression.

Dr. Nathanson's film leaves a similar impression, which explains why the liberal media, the same media which dwells on the plight on helpless animals, will not pay any attention to a film that brings viewers face to face with the horror of abortion and forces them to think rather than to simply strike what they regard as the right—the trendy—attitude.

Fetus Feels Pain

This film using new sonographic techniques, shows the outline of the child in the womb thrashing to resist the suction device before it tears off the head. Then you see the dead child dismembered and the head crushed. Then the parts are sucked out. . . .

Nobody who sees this film will speak again of ''painless'' abortion. The doctor who performed the abortion couldn't bear to watch the film to the end. He rushed out of the room where it was shown and never performed another ''procedure,'' though he had performed several thousand before.

Joseph Sobran, *Conservative Digest*, August 1984.

The success of the pro-choice movement can be attributed largely to the way the media has treated the abortion question. By keeping the public in the dark, the most influential newspapers have participated in a conspiracy of silence that allows otherwise intelligent and compassionate people to accept at face value the cliches of the pro-choice movement.

The pro-choice movement has also been aided immeasurably by the perception that only cranks oppose abortion. The liberal media is largely responsible for creating that impression. Feminist columnists, such as the [Boston] Globe's Ellen Goodman, are at best patronizing and at worst openly scornful of anyone who speaks out against abortion. Thus the uninformed public tends to shy away from the issue, lest they be branded as Bible-thumping rednecks or Roman Catholics blindly obedient to whatever decree is issued by the Vatican.

Dr. Nathanson can be classified as neither. As a highly-respected physician and a founding member of NARAL, it is reasonable to assume that he enlisted in the pro-life movement for one reason only—and that is to stop the wanton killing of tiny beings who are fully capable of experiencing the terror and pain that accompanies their death. One such death is shown in Dr. Nathanson's ultrasound film, for which he provides the following commentary:

"You can see from the moment the tip of the suction machine starts to move, the fetus knows it and starts to scuttle to the top of the uterus. You can see her mouth open in a silent scream. From there on you can see all the agitation: you can see the heart speeding up, you can see the limbs moving faster, you can see the child moving more rapidly. Even the breathing increases. So there is no question this child feels pain, and actually senses danger."

"The Silent Scream insists that it depicts a murder . . . the claim makes the film emotionally powerful, so powerful in fact that it undermines the pro-life position it is supposed to advance."

The Film's Tactics Prove the Fetus Is Not Fully Human

Jefferson Morley

Jefferson Morley is associate editor of *The New Republic*, a weekly journal of opinion. He believes that while the film does "convincingly demonstrate that the fetus is a living being with human attributes," the film's emotional impact necessitates a probe of its intent. By allowing a murder to take place on-screen, the pro-lifers are either insidiously immoral, producing the equivalent of a snuff film, or actually admitting that this life is not fully human.

As you read, consider the following questions:

1. What two things does the film prove, according to the author?
2. What argument does the author give to dismantle the pro-lifers' assertion that abortion is equivalent to a holocaust?
3. What is the real issue in the abortion debate, according to Mr. Morley?

The Silent Scream has the appeal of a snuff movie. Its notoriety, like that of the controversial porno films of a few years ago in which unknown actresses were ostensibly killed on camera, derives from the uncertainty about whether the viewer is witnessing the actual murder of a human being. The already-famous film, which pro-life groups have screened at the White House and distributed to every member of Congress, features an apparently unprecedented visual depiction of a sonic scan of a woman's womb during an abortion. But while snuff films held out the possibility of murder in order to titillate the trenchcoat crowd inured to every other variety of immorality, *The Silent Scream* insists that it depicts a murder in order to outrage a public that now tolerates abortion. The unequivocal claim makes the film emotionally powerful, so powerful in fact that it undermines the pro-life position it is supposed to advance.

The film builds its case slowly. After the inappropriate horror B-movie title rolls, the narrator, Dr. Bernard Nathanson, appears. Nathanson is a former abortionist who says he presided over 60,000 abortions at his New York City clinic in the mid-1970s. He explains how knowledge about the human fetus has grown rapidly. Black-and-white footage of a well-developed fetus is shown. It is moving slightly with its thumb apparently in its mouth. "The unborn child," Nathanson says, "is simply another human being, another member of the human community, indistinguishable in every way from any of us."

The Film's Tension Increases

Nathanson returns with a lineup of seven plastic models, each of a fetus at different stages of development. Our identification with the humanity of this fetus is supposed to grow with these models. Then we cut to the antiseptic interior of an abortion clinic, where an unidentifiable woman lies on a table with her legs spread. Nathanson explains how the abortionist dilates the cervix to gain access to the womb. The juxtaposition works; the film begins to make you uneasy.

As the sonogram is shown again, Nathanson says that what will follow is typical of the 4,000 abortions done every day in the United States. He points out the head of the fetus, its eyes, its ribs. Its heart is beating 140 times a minute, he says. The details are hard to discern in what looks to me like a satellite weather photo. But with Nathanson's explanations, it's not hard to picture the human characteristics of the fetus.

There is a flash across the screen. Nathanson says that this is the abortionist's instrument probing for the fetus. The instrument, he explains, has been colored so that it will show up on film. There is movement. Nathanson says that the fetus, sensing the intrusion, has recoiled. Its heartbeat has increased. He claims its mouth is open to scream. When the abortion is over, Nathanson concludes, "All we see remaining are simply the shards, the broken fragments, the pieces of tissue which document there was once a living defenseless tiny human being here."

A Snuff Film

What we have seen is disturbing, but not only for the reasons Nathanson intends. For anyone who didn't know it, *The Silent Scream* demonstrates convincingly that a fetus is a living being with human attributes. But the film proves too much. If what we have seen was exactly like the killing of a defenseless human being, why did Nathanson stand by and watch it? Would it be morally acceptable for Mike Wallace to go on the set of a snuff film and tape an acutal murder so that "60 Minutes" could ignite public outrage about the practice?

I recognize that this is an ugly kind of argument I am making. Such casual talk of killing people, all too common in contemporary political calculations, is repulsive. I develop this point precisely because *The Silent Scream* allows us no choice. And not to follow the argument of *The Silent Scream* to its logical conclusion is not to take the film or the anti-abortion movement seriously.

Nathanson might respond to the "60 Minutes" analogy by saying something like this: because abortion is legal, making the sonogram was the most I could do without interfering with the woman's (current) right to have an abortion. But this will hardly

AHA!! HOLDING HANDS! THAT'S THE BEGINNING OF LIFE — NEXT THING WE KNOW SHE'LL WANT AN ABORTION!"

do. If the United States government, by allowing legal abortions, is now condoning 4,000 murders a day, civil disobedience, if not armed rebellion, would certainly be called for. If 4,000 illegal immigrants or 4,000 homosexuals or 4,000 Republicans were being killed each day, we like to think we would protest—and more vigorously than just by holding peaceful vigils outside the concentration camps.

Indeed in such a horrific society, non-violent resistance would constitute—like pacifism in the face of Nazi genocide—a profound moral failing. The most admirable response would be to organize a clandestine violent opposition to hinder if not end the mass murder. Anyone who firebombed Belsen would have been, in our judgment today, a hero, not an "extremist." Thus the people who firebomb abortion clinics are at least being true to the message of *The Silent Scream*. They are the only ones who, in the midst of what some anti-abortion groups call the "American Holocaust," are not acting like good Germans.

Abortion as Murder Not Serious

By disowning the bombers, the anti-abortion movement reveals it does not take its own rhetoric as seriously as it wants the public to do. And Nathanson's appearance in the film is devastatingly ironic confirmation of the point. By his own admission he has overseen the killing of 60,000 "member[s] of the human community, indistinguishable in every way from any of us." Nathanson has criticized other anti-abortionists for resorting facilely to the Nazi analogy, but he cannot escape responsibility for his own language. If we take him at his word, he has committed crimes on the magnitude of a Nazi war criminal. If we take *The Silent Scream* as literally as its sponsors say we must, we can have but one conclusion: Dr. [Josef] Mengele has emerged from the Paraguayan bush and, citing what he learned at Dachau, is fervently urging us to support the Universal Declaration of Human Rights. And his testimony has been warmly welcomed at the White House.

This, of course, is preposterous. We can be sure Nathanson does not think of himself as the moral equivalent of a war criminal, his own rhetoric notwithstanding. Similarly, we can be sure President Reagan does not really believe he presides over a country as murderous as Nazi Germany. (Talk about blaming America first.) Reagan and Nathanson can live with themselves only by absolving themselves from the indictment of their own logic. They can only retain our respect by conceding that abortion is not murder.

This doesn't destroy the anti-abortion case. It merely makes it debatable. The double irony of *The Silent Scream* is that Nathanson himself has persuasively made this point. In 1979 he wrote *Aborting America*, an honest and thoughtful book about his conversion to the anti-abortion cause. "What are we to call the entity that lies at the heart of the debate?" he asked. He rejected "unborn baby or unborn child," saying that "the anti-abortionists would load the verbal dice on us" by using these terms. "We are not here talking about the type of life that we find in a six year old," Nathanson wrote then. "It certainly is biological life, but life of a different order." He also wrote, "We are not talking about intentional and unjustified slaying of a human being." The word "murder," he said, "should be dropped from the abortion issue, along with 'killing' and 'homocide.' "

Propaganda at Its Finest

What is important to keep in mind while viewing *The Silent Scream* is that it is propaganda at its finest: the kind of emotional, dramatic propaganda that haunts our hearts and minds, and serves, quite cleverly, to cloud an already cloudy issue.

Anita Creamer, *St. Paul Pioneer Press*, April 21, 1985.

Nathanson's general point in *Aborting America* was that life is a continuum from conception on. The fetus might be life of a different order, he argued, but as life it deserved as much protection as possible. This is a fair point. But it is equally logical to contend that "life of a different order" can be treated differently than human life.

Here the lines of the abortion debate are clear. The anti-abortion camp believes that this different order of life is still so close to human that a pregnant woman should under almost no circumstances—or no circumstances at all—eliminate it. The pro-abortion movement believes that a woman should not be required to subordinate other aspects of her life to the needs of a being that is not fully human. In deciding on abortion, these are the two positions we must choose between, a choice that *The Silent Scream* almost succeeds in obscuring.

a critical thinking skill

Distinguishing Between Fact and Opinion

This activity is designed to help develop the basic reading and thinking skill of distinguishing between fact and opinion. Consider the following statement as an example: "Abortion is the act of terminating a pregnancy." This statement is a fact with which few people would disagree. But consider a statement which casts an opinion about abortion. "Abortion is the taking of a human life and therefore immoral." Such a statement is clearly an expressed opinion. Many people who are against abortion might agree, but to those who believe abortion is justified, this statement is inaccurate.

When investigating controversial issues it is important to be able to distinguish between statements which are stated as fact and those which are clearly statements of opinion.

The following statements are taken from the viewpoints in this chapter. Consider each statement carefully. *Mark O for any statement you feel is an opinion or an interpretation of facts. Mark F for any statement you believe is a fact. Mark N for any statement you believe is too controversial to decide.*

If you are doing this activity as a member of a class or group, compare your answers with those of other class or group members. Be able to defend your answers. You may discover that others will come to different conclusions than you. Listening to the reasons others present for their answers may give you valuable insights in distinguishing between fact and opinion.

If you are reading this book alone, ask others if they agree with your answers. You too will find this interaction very valuable.

O = opinion
F = fact
N = too controversial to decide

1. Human life begins at conception.

2. If a pregnancy is not terminated, a baby will be born.

3. An ova and a sperm do not constitute human life.

4. If you call a fertilized egg a human life, then every other cell in the body can be called a human life.

5. Genetically, hormonally and in all organic respects save for the source of its nourishment, a fetus and even an embryo, is separate from the woman.

6. An embryo is just a blob of tissue.

7. Biological man is the product of forty-six chromosomes that combine to create a unique identity at the time an egg is fertilized by a sperm.

8. The possession of forty-six chromosomes does not make a cell a person.

9. A woman's rights overshadow the rights of the fetus.

10. Abortion is legal.

11. The Catholic church believes abortion is wrong under any circumstances except to save the life of the mother.

12. To be a person, there must be evidence of personality.

13. Physicians can now perform operations on a fetus in the womb.

14. Fetal surgery has proven the fetus is a human being.

15. What is at issue for women who have abortions is the quality of their lives.

16. Nearly eighty percent of abortions occur within the first ten weeks of pregnancy.

17. A fetus is viable when it can live outside the womb.

18. Abortion after the twentieth week of pregnancy should not be allowed.

19. A twelve-week old fetus cannot feel pain.

Periodical Bibliography

The following list of periodical articles deals with the subject matter of this chapter.

David Cannon	"Abortion and Infanticide," *Policy Review*, Spring 1985.
Stephen L. Carter	"Roe vs. Wade Left Both Sides Open to Science," *The Wall Street Journal*, August 11, 1985.
Ronald K.L. Collins	"If Fetuses Are Persons, Then . . .," *Los Angeles Times*, August 16, 1985.
John Jefferson Davis	"When Does Personhood Begin?" *Eternity*, November 1979.
Philip Hager	"Medical Gains Stir Debate on Abortion Ruling," *Los Angeles Times*, September 9, 1985.
Nat Hentoff	"If It's Not a Human Being, What's the Crime?" *Village Voice*, March 6, 1984.
Russell T. Hitt	"Left to Die: When Late-Term Abortions Fail," *Eternity*, March 1985.
Dena Kleiman	"When Abortion Becomes Birth: A Dilemma of Medical Ethics Shaken by New Advances," *The New York Times*, February 15, 1984.
Robert W. Lee	"The Silent Scream of Abortion," *American Opinion*, May 1985.
Elizabeth Mehren	"A Refutation of 'Silent Scream,' " *Los Angeles Times*, March 25, 1985.
The New Republic	"Right-To-Life Porn," March 25, 1985.
Joseph Sobran	"The Averted Gaze: Liberalism and Fetal Pain," *The Human Life Review*, Spring 1984. Available from 150 E. Thirty-fifth St., New York, NY 10016.
Ellen Willis	"Putting Women Back into the Abortion Debate," *Village Voice*, July 16, 1985.

Should Abortion Remain a Personal Choice?

VIEWPOINT 1

"When the day comes that the decision to bear a child for all women is a moral choice . . . then and only then, the human liberation of women will be a reality."

Abortion Should Be a Woman's Personal Choice

Beverly Wildung Harrison

Whether abortion and birth control should be a woman's decision has been a source of controversy throughout history. Prochoice advocates claim that since the fetus develops inside a woman's body, it should be her prerogative to abort. In the following viewpoint, Beverly Wildung Harrison supports this view. Only by allowing the abortion decision to completely remain the woman's, she argues, can we achieve an ethical and moral society. A professor of Christian Ethics at Union Theological Seminary in New York, Ms. Harrison writes widely and lectures frequently on social ethics and the ethics of procreative choice. She is past president of the Society of Christian Ethics.

As you read, consider the following questions:

1. Why does the author believe it is inconsistent for conservatives to be against legal abortion?
2. How does abortion provide a good experience for teenage women, according to the author?
3. Why does the author believe abortion to be an essential freedom for women?

Two separate and antagonistic ideological trends threaten women's capacity to come to grips with the morality of abortion and to formulate an adequate ethic of procreative choice. Addressing the moral meaning of procreative choice in women's lives is the necessary prelude to the evaluation of abortion. Yet sensibilities widely shared by two different groups of women militate against our entering into crucial dialogue on this issue and launching the task of moral reconceptualization. It is necessary, therefore, to unravel the tensions that make it difficult for women to bring abortion into focus as a moral question prior to reconceiving the morality of procreative choice.

One concern, widely voiced by men but also by some women relatively unalienated by the presumed "traditional" role of motherhood, is that any critique of dominant Christian teaching, including abortion ethics, is hostile not only toward men but also toward those women who choose and value marriage and motherhood as central to their lives. The propagandistic claims of the political New Right, cultivating and playing on such fears, have been packaged to convince women that the women's movement agenda, including the pro-choice stance, poses a serious threat to their identity and lifestyle. There are, after all, millions of women in our society who, if they regret anything about their own life choices, certainly do not regret their decision to use their procreative power, personal energies, and creativity to bear children and to make a home for a family.

Condemnation of Feminism

It is hard for many people, including women whose energies have been directed toward motherhood and homemaking, to entertain the possibility that this process of discrediting feminism *is itself an intentional effort to divert the pace of social change away from greater justice for all women.* The multifaceted pressures generated by the women's movement in the last decade have gone well beyond the demand that women receive equal pay for equal work. Feminism spawned the much more radical notion that women's bodies and all of women's work—including housework and child care—should be valued as much as men's lives and work are valued. The effects of these convictions, translated into social practice, would be sufficient to threaten the existing structures of privilege and patterns of distribution of wealth in this society. Hence the need among dominant males and the women they have subjugated to turn back these demands for deep and genuine social equality for women. This leads to the "put-down" of a full, consistent women's liberation agenda. It is important to appreciate in this connection the extent to which procreative choice, and legal abortion as its guarantor, is fundamental to all other justice claims that women make. Failure to see this point may mean a major historical setback for women's struggle for justice. If the availability of safe, legal abortion can be isolated and split off as somehow a "more radical" issue than, for example, the Equal Rights Amendment, women who advocate social equality will witness the very effective derailment of their long-term agenda. It is crucial to develop the understanding that women's support for a so-called pro-life social policy option has the objective result of placing unbearable pressure on other women whose life situations are less favorable, if more typical of the lot of women generally. Many women, however, will change neither their moral position about abortion nor their attitudes toward abortion politics until they are persuaded that a pro-choice position is grounded in a deeper, stronger, more caring moral vision than the anti-abortion political option now articulated with such apparent ethical passion. The outlook of many women who do not yet see the moral wisdom of a pro-choice social policy, for them as well as for all women, will change only as we attempt to adequately frame our case for procreative choice as a moral claim.

Traditional Mothers and Choice

The women who embrace and celebrate their own and other women's devotion to childbearing have little difficulty appreciating why abortion is a moral issue, because they recognize and cherish

the deep and fundamental values at stake in these decisions. However much some of these women may fail to recognize the extent of social injustice toward women as a group, they well understand and sympathize with the claim that the abortion controversy is a moral one. It is not surprising that they sometimes identify with public leaders who favor curtailing legal abortion, because such politicians frequently mask their position by moral appeals to "family values." The conviction of the "more traditional" women that abortion is a moral issue can be a strong resource for our collective struggle to formulate an adequate ethic of reproductive freedom, provided that we all clarify the concrete connections between procreative choice and social well-being. Whenever we forget traditional women's sensitivity to the value of childbearing and nurturing, we make it harder to reach these women, who are so important to the cause of procreative choice. It is they, after all, who have had the greatest actual degree of experience with the *benefits* of procreative choice. Many such women have received the strong family and social support for the positive exercise of procreative power that makes childbearing and childrearing a joyful experience.

Government Control

It would be naive, however, to imagine that powerful interests in this society wish women to possess the power of genuine procreative choice. All present proposals for a so-called pro-life (or anti-abortion) social policy involve making the state the controller of procreation. This social policy of state control of women's procreative power almost invariably is favored precisely by people otherwise professing the ideology that state interference in the "private" lives of citizens is wrong! Furthermore, zeal for increased military spending and for capital punishment more often than not thrives among legislators most eager to prevent all legal abortion. Nothing makes clearer how little women count as full, valued persons or as competent moral agents than this dramatic ideological inconsistency on the part of so many anti-abortion advocates. On the one hand they endorse unquestioningly a laissez-faire economic doctrine that assumes (decades of contrary experience notwithstanding) that unrestricted economic activity produces optimal social welfare and that state intervention in the economy for the purpose of justice is a great evil. Simultaneously they insist that the state must intervene to secure sexual conformity and, above all, "procreative morality"—that is, to control women's distinctive social power. This selective ideology about the role of the state is characteristic of many leaders in this society, who espouse whatever social ideology is necessary to justify the perpetuation of their power. It is also critical that women recognize how the active discrediting of the women's movement works to suppress women's potential to work together for all social change, not merely to control procreation. What feminism is and always has been about is *expanding the concrete range of choices available to all women*—to women as a group and to women as individuals.

We must understand, as we discuss the ethics of procreative choice and the morality of abortion, the connection between women's subjugation, historically, and the efforts of male-dominated social institutions and systems to control the critical human social power of procreation. Women's emancipation depends personally and collectively on how societies choose to shape this power. We cannot eschew a feminist analysis without obscuring the real meaning and moral significance of the controversy at hand. As feminist scholars have begun the long, slow, and difficult task of reconstructing the real but suppressed history of women's contribution to human culture and society, it has become evident that in most societies frequent, fundamental social tension has existed between women's and men's cultures precisely over the issue of fertility control. . . .

Women Need the Abortion Option

I think feminists have been so traumatized by the fundamentalist crusade against abortion and all the talk of fetuses and when life begins that they are in danger of forgetting the values that made abortion a feminist issue in the first place. Underneath the hysteria, poll after poll shows that the great majority of women in this nation, and most men, still want to decide when and whether to have a child in accordance with their own conscience. . . .

I think women who are young, and those not so young, today must be able to choose when to have a child, given the necessities of their jobs. They will indeed join their mothers, who remember the humiliations and dangers of back-street butcher abortions, in a march of millions to save the right of legal abortion.

Betty Friedan, *The New York Times Magazine*, November 3, 1985.

Women, who may make diverse life choices about their procreative power, still need to unite in appreciation of what they have in common. However they view their own biological fertility, freedom in their lives will have no concrete meaning apart from the socially supported conditions that enable them to shape that fertility. Furthermore, a genuine degree of freedom from coercion is important to every woman. This principle of noncoercion could be as critical for women who wish to center their lives in childbearing as for those who do not. . . .

Perhaps this is why women, despite their strong identification with motherhood, always reveal some ambivalence in studies that give them an opportunity to confidentially disclose their real feelings about childbearing. A considerable number of women acknowledge some regret about *whatever* choices they make. And because the formidable social construction of women's lives beckons us to "celebrate motherhood," only later in life do myriad women recognize that their childbearing was not chosen, that it was the result of pervasive social pressure that, they see in retrospect, they had no ability to refuse at the time. No one can deny that traditional female socialization tends to undermine a woman's capacity to know clearly what she wants for herself. Women frequently drift into motherhood only to discover after the fact the high social cost of mothering. This does not mean that such women regret having borne their children. Most live into their ambivalence and overcome it. Many young women also experience their first, life-changing coming of age when they find themselves unexpectedly pregnant; for many, pregnancy is their first genuine and realistic encounter with adult reality. That some women's first real awareness of the need to take charge of their lives, in the face of very limited social options, comes from unwanted pregnancy is sad. Such psychological innocence is rooted both in female socialization and in young women's social powerlessness. Support for developing psychological maturity is no easier for women, even affluent women, to achieve than is support for social justice. We have reason to be grateful that safe, legal abortion provides at least the *negative* means of assuring the elements of choice, given that far too may of us must still drift into maturity through crisis surrounding our procreative capacity.

The Morality of Choice

To defend the morality of procreative choice for women is not to deny reverence toward or appreciation for many women's deep commitment to childbearing and child nurturance. It does ask that women collectively come to understand that genuine choice with respect to procreative power (not simply choice for the sake of choice) is a necessary condition of *any and all* women's human fulfillment. When the day comes that the decision to bear a child, for all women, is a moral choice—that is, a deliberated, thoughtful decision to act for the enhancement of our own and our society's well-being with full responsibility for all the implications of that action—then and only then, the human liberation of women will be a reality.

2 VIEWPOINT

"The choice ethic has trivialized the choice to abort."

Abortion Should Not Be a Woman's Personal Choice

Frank S. Zepezauer

Those who believe abortion should not be a personal choice argue that the fetus is a separate entity from the woman who carries it, and therefore entitled to the right to live. They believe that women who choose to abort do so primarily out of convenience, a fact which trivializes unborn human life. In the following viewpoint, Frank Zepezauer takes this argument a step further, arguing that the "choice ethic" of the pro-abortionists denies any humanity to the fetus at all, a stance that shows an utter lack of moral character. A California high school teacher, Mr. Zepezauer is a frequent contributor to *The Human Life Review* and many other American journals.

As you read, consider the following questions:

1. How does the author relate "The Road Not Taken," to abortion?
2. What evidence does the author give to prove his statement that society hates children? Do you believe he is right?
3. The author claims that there are more options in the abortion issue than fifteen years ago, and he does not approve of this. Why?

Frank S. Zepezauer, "The Choice Ethic," *The Human Life Review*, Winter/Spring 1985. Reprinted with the author's permission.

Two roads diverged in a yellow wood,
And sorry I could not travel both
And be one traveller, long I stood
And looked down one as far as I could
To where it bent in the undergrowth;

Then took the other, as just as fair,
And having perhaps the better claim,
Because it was grassy and wanted wear;
Though as for that the passing there
Had worn them really about the same,

And both that morning equally lay
In leaves no step had trodden black.
Oh, I kept the first for another day!
Yet knowing how way leads on to way,
I doubted if I should ever come back.

I shall be telling this with a sigh
Somewhere ages and ages hence:
Two roads diverged in a wood, and I—
I took the one less traveled by,
And that has made all the difference.

The Road Not Taken
Robert Frost

Frost's poem once served as an anthem to an individualism shaped and hardened by significant choice. Yet today it transmits an antique sound. Its words repeat a value whose substance has been lost to a new ethic which subordinates motive and result and shared standards to choice itself. It weakens the kind of choice we call commitment, deprives many other choices of moral meaning and encourages a statism that will deny choice altogether.

The Road Not Taken reminds us of the commitment we now try to restore. The narrator studied two equally attractive alternatives, regretted he could not take both, and then chose one and stayed with it. His choice thus distinguished between essential and contingent decisions. Choosing one road meant that every choice thereafter was guided by the determination to stick with the first fundamental choice. Chance and circumstance thus always confronted basic conviction. Circumstance opened to him life's rich possibilities and conviction shut him into its limitations. You take one road and soon way leads to way and other roads fade into memory. Life is a feast, but you can't have it all.

For many women in the past, and for a stubborn remnant today, pregnancy also chanced upon basic commitment. A being came alive in the womb, a fact for which an earlier choice shaped responsible adaptations, what you must do to continue on your chosen road. But today the maternal mind labors with a different problem: not how to stay with your fundamental choice but how to choose between two new alternatives. And while these options confound the response to pregancy, commitment is put on hold.

Tentativeness postpones action.

A feminist newspaperwoman, Joan Beck, has quarreled with this maybe yes-maybe no style of pregnancy. Like most people who studied embryology, she sees a human where her liberationist sisters see disposable protoplasm. She sees in this "mindset" not only obvious danger to the "unwanted" child, but hazards as well to the lucky survivors who found themselves for a while in a mother who had not yet make up her mind whether she wanted to *be* a mother. If, from the beginning, a woman's mind has set for itself the identity of "mother"—a fixed condition with clear responsibilities—she will live with the recognition that another life now makes a claim on her own. Every habit, whim or choice. . .thought and feeling itself. . .will be guided by accepted reality. What she eats or drinks or smokes, breathes in, injects or swallows. . .each will be tested by the needs of the child growing within her. If those needs must wait until further decision, they might receive indifferent attention if they are met at all. You don't prepare very well for dinner guests while you're still deciding to invite them. . . .

The Choice Ethic

Now that the choice ethic transforms each surviving child into a privileged member of the increasingly exclusive club of humans, we now find fewer and fewer of them and treat them with less

Reprinted by permission: Tribune Media Services.

and less hospitality. We seem to hate the children we so generously "want." We consign many of them to nannies or to day care centers, hoping they'll find enough commitment to subordinate greed, incompetence and bureaucratic apathy. We hand them latch keys and feed their boundless curiosity with two hundred square inches of dancing electrons. We abandon them to the reciprocating confusions of their peer group and the isolating distortions of their fantasies. We bounce them between warring ex-spouses. We batter and abuse and sexually molest them. We alienate them from their grandparents. We cut them off from their family histories. We drag them into ad hoc alternative families with shifting memberships. We see a million of them a year running away from home, many thousands killing themselves, thousands more killing their spirits. Even when we work to strengthen our marriages and protect our families, we find whole sections of our cities out of bounds to families with children and tax laws that favor the dual-income aristocrats of Yuppieland. Is the choice ethic to blame for all of this? Perhaps not, but an ethic that makes children and spouses and two-parent households increasingly hostage to choice eventually denies them the commitment needed to sustain them. To what can you commit yourself except to more choice or to the Self whose needs the choice-maker primarily consults? . . .

An Indulgence of Will

When the choice to abort a child or a marriage does not confront two roughly balanced alternatives, it becomes instead a bowing to the obvious or an indulgence of the will. The constant reference, even today, of the hard cases that opened the way to the abortion freedom—the desperate unmarried woman, the rape or incest victim, the potentially damaged child, the physically endangered mother—recall the time when destroying the unborn was a weighty undertaking which demanded an accounting. It had to be argued that what was killed was indeed a baby whose continued existence nevertheless, in those special circumstances, had become the greater of two evils.

But the choice ethic has trivialized the choice to abort. To kill or not to kill a human being, that was indeed a weighty question, productive sometimes of even heroic choice. But to rid oneself of a cellular intrusion in a procedure as ordinary as wart sanding or to choose between a blob of protoplasm and an Interrupted Career, barely qualifies as choice, only embracing the obvious. The pro-abortionist argument that many women still do, in fact, anguish over their choice still defers to obsolescent values fading behind an emerging value which permits any abortion for any reason. We can hope every destroyed child loses his life to a solemn decision thoroughly debated, but we can't demand it nor can we demand a public accounting because "private choice" has become as privileged as a tabernacle. Thus we play "let's pretend" and assume that the drama of the hard cases is re-enacted every year in one million and five hundred thousand abortions, or worse: that the choice to kill a child was the result of a solemn deliberation simply *because* the women chose to kill. The choice itself gives weight to the decision, not the reasons that prompted it. . . .

Frost said in his poem that his choice—the one he took and held and grew by—although less traveled by, "made all the difference." The distance we've traveled into the choice ethic will also make all the difference because those who follow us might not have the chance to choose at all.

VIEWPOINT 3

"Abortion is far too important to be left up to a woman and her doctor."

Men Should Take Part in the Abortion Decision

Bill Stout

While abortion is primarily thought of as a woman's issue, many men believe this perspective should change. In the following viewpoint, Bill Stout remembers the painful and traumatic experience of his wife's abortion, and comes to the conclusion that men's feelings should be recognized and acknowledged in the abortion decision. A nationally-known CBS network correspondent for many years, Mr. Stout currently does TV commentary for station KCBS in Los Angeles.

As you read, consider the following questions:

1. Why was his wife's decision to have an abortion so traumatic for the author?
2. Why was the author confused by his wife's decision?

Bill Stout, "He (or She) Would Be 23," *The Human Life Review*, Summer 1976. Reprinted with the author's permission.

Doctors and theologians are usually the only men who argue the abortion issue. Mostly, it's a women's debate. On one side: "We have the right to control our own bodies," and on the other: "It's a human life and killing it is wrong." That sort of thing.

But I had a jolt recently that sent me thinking seriously, *personally*, about abortion for the first time in more than 20 years. I suspect it was a shock that has hit a great many men, although few ever talk about it.

It came late on a Friday afternoon, at the start of a long holiday weekend. The freeways were jammed, of course, and when I started out for a business meeting on the far side of Los Angeles, the radio was full of "sigalerts." Since there was plenty of time, it seemed logical to skip the freeway mess and loaf across the city on the side streets. Easy enough, until even that oozing pace of traffic squeezed to a dead stop because of an accident at the corner of Beverly and Vermont. There my eye caught the window of a second floor office, and it hit me like a knee in the groin.

That office, in a building I hadn't even noticed in many years, was where I had taken my new bride for an abortion one blistering summer day in 1952. Suddenly I remembered . . . and I relived every detail.

We had been married two years and did not consider ourselves poor, but we were close. We had an old car, a few dollars in the bank, and I had a temporary job writing news stories for radio announcers. And she was pregnant.

Arguing for a Week

We had argued for more than a week after her first cautious announcement. I had adopted her young son by a previous marriage, but this would be our first baby together, and I was delighted. Minutes later I was appalled, then infuriated, by her insistence she would not go through with it. Even more hurtful, I suppose, in the callowness of that encounter so long ago, was that she had talked with several women friends before telling me anything. She already had the name of the doctor and was ready to make an appointment when I would be off from work to drive her to and from.

There was a lot of shouting and pleading that week and a good deal of pumping up (by me) of my prospects at the radio station. She pointed out that those were prospects only. She noted the sickly condition of our bankbook, plus the fact that we had 12 payments to go on our first television set. She also made the point hammered home today by the women's pro-abortion groups: it was, after all, *her* body, and the *decision* should be hers and hers alone.

That was the most painful week of our marriage, until the final anguish (of divorce) many years later. Of course, she got her way.

I dropped her at the curb outside the doctor's office then pulled around the corner to park and wait. It would be forty-five minutes, she said, no more than an hour at most. She had $200 in cash in her bag. No checks were accepted.

I spent the time multiplying and dividing. How much did this doctor *make* per hour? Per minute? How many of these jobs could he do in a day? Or in a year? Did he take just a two-week vacation so he could hurry back to the women with so many different reasons for ending pregnancies?

I remember his name. I can see the sign in his office window as clearly as if it were there now, just a few feet away. Seven letters, four in the first name; below them, centered on a separate line, "M.D." I never saw the man but I hated him then, and do to this moment, even though he died long ago.

Nothing to Talk About

When I saw her come out of his office, pale and wincing with each step, I leaped out of the car and ran to her. A couple of days later she was moving around with her usual energy and she made it clear that it was all over, with nothing to talk about. A year and a half later, with everything going fine for me in my work, she gave birth to our first baby, a normal healthy boy, and not long after that there came a daughter.

"I Want to Help Decide"

So far no one seems to have come up with any better alternative than simply making an abortion decision more palatable to a man. Some abortion counselors are trying harder than ever to encourage men to discuss their frustrations and to explore what the experience means to them.

The inadequacies of the approach are obvious. "I don't want someone to hold my hand and say they're sorry," said the man who stood silently by for his girlfriend's abortion. "I want to have a chance to help decide."

Patricia O'Brien, *St. Paul Pioneer Press*, October 13, 1983.

Yet, again and again, I have found myself wondering what that first one would have been like. A boy or a girl? Blonde or brunette? A problem or a delight? Whatever kind of person the lost one might have been, I feel even now that we had no right to take its life. Religion has nothing to do with that feeling. It was a "gut" response that overwhelmed me while stalled in the traffic that afternoon at Beverly and Vermont.

Now we were moving again. A few minutes later I was at my meeting in the Civic Center, in the office of an old friend, luckily, because by then I was in tears and they wouldn't stop. It wasn't easy but I finally told him how that glance at an office window had simply been too much for me, sweeping away a dam that had held for more than 20 years.

Haunting Feelings

If I am still wondering about the first one that never was, what about other men? How many of them share my haunted feeling about children who might have been? Why are we, the fathers who never were, so reluctant to talk about such feelings? And if it can be so painful for the men, how much worse must if be for the women who nurture and then give up the very fact of life itself?

Clearly, as the saying goes about wars and generals, abortion is far too important to be left to a woman and her doctor.

4 VIEWPOINT

"Abortion is still a woman's right, a woman's choice. When a man and a woman cannot come to agreement, it is the woman's wish that must prevail."

A Man's Involvement Is of Secondary Importance

Kathleen McDonnell

Kathleen McDonnell has written extensively on women's health and other issues for a number of Canadian magazines. She also writes fiction and is the author of three plays. *Not an Easy Choice: A Feminist Re-Examines Abortion*, from which this viewpoint is excerpted, is her first book. In it, Ms. McDonnell concedes that when possible, women should include the man in the abortion decision. However, when a man and woman disagree over abortion, or when the woman decides she does not want to involve the man, the ultimate decision should be hers.

As you read, consider the following questions:

1. What is the most common male response to unwanted pregnancy, according to the author?
2. Why does the author believe that men should be included in the abortion decision?
3. Under what circumstances, does the author argue, should men be excluded from the abortion decision?

Kathleen McDonnell, *Not an Easy Choice: A Feminist Re-Examines Abortion*. Boston: South End Press, 1984. Reprinted with the permission of Women's Press, Toronto.

While some criticize feminists for ignoring the fetus in the abortion issue, others (often the same people) do so for ignoring men as well. And indeed, with our steady insistence that "abortion is a woman's right," we may sometimes forget, or appear to forget, that abortion always occurs in the context of sexual contact between a woman and a man. (Except, of course, in the rare case of an abortion where the pregnancy is the result of artificial insemination. Even then there is male involvement, but not *sexual* involvement.)

Often the man is no longer in the picture by the time the abortion takes place, or the woman has chosen not to tell the man that she is pregnant, or she may not even know for certain who the father is. But whether or not the man is present within the orbit of persons and events surrounding an abortion, the fact remains that men as a group are intimately and inextricably connected to abortion. Like making a baby, it takes two to create an unwanted pregnancy.

In dealing with abortion and other reproductive matters, feminists have gone a long way toward eradicating the sexist notion that unwanted pregnancy is the fault of the woman, a kind of punishment for sexual activity that men are not expected to share. But while fostering the notion that men should bear an equal share of responsibility in reproductive matters, feminists have been reluctant to accord them anything more than a minor role in reproductive decisions, especially where abortion is concerned. There are some perfectly good reasons for this. Women are the ones who bear children. Women are the ones, still, who are largely responsible for their care and nurturing. It is our bodies and our lives that are at issue, so the decisions must be ours as well. Besides, ample evidence over the centuries has shown us that we have been prudent not to accord men much say in reproductive matters, expecially abortion, because on the whole they have not acquitted themselves well in this area.

Men and Abortion

The most common male response to unwanted pregnancy when it occurs outside of marriage has been to "take off," leaving the woman to bear the physical, the emotional and, often, the financial brunt of either having an abortion or carrying the pregnancy to term. Studies of abortion and its aftermath reveal that, more often than not, relationships do not survive an abortion: the majority of unmarried couples break up either before or soon after an abortion. In many cases, of course, the breakup is at the instigation of the woman, or the decision is a mutual one. But the most frequent scenario is that the man terminates the relationship on being told of the pregnancy or shortly after the abortion, or he just gradually fades out of the picture. Male reluctance to accept responsibility in reproductive matters extends far beyond pregnancy and abortion, of course. The majority of men still regard the use of contraception as a woman's problem, for example. And men are increasingly disowning responsibility for their own biological children, as Barbara Ehrenreich demonstrates in her book *The Hearts of Men.* Over the past decade and a half men have begun to "take off" in unprecedented numbers, abandoning their traditional breadwinner roles, defaulting on support payments and leaving women to be the sole financial support of their children.

Male-Dominated Society

I think I am only beginning to understand, as a man, why women are driven to the desperate violence of taking life in their wombs—in a society where men accept virtually no responsibility for their sexuality with women or for the personal care of their own children.

Jim Douglass, *Sojourners,* November 1980.

Often men take the opposite tack when confronted with an unplanned pregnancy: they stick around and demand that the woman not abort "their" child. This demand is rarely accompanied by an offer to raise and support the child, however. Personal accounts of abortion reveal this particular scenario with an astounding frequency: the man will say he is "against abortion" or forbid the woman to abort "his" child, without the slightest awareness of the responsibility that this position logically demands of him. A woman in one study even felt that her lover was "more logical and more correct" in his contention that "she should have the child and raise it without either his presence or his financial support." Another, a fifteen-year-old, acceded to her boyfriend's wish not to "murder his child." But after she decided against having an abortion, he left her to raise the child alone and "ruined my life," she said.

Proving Their Virility

This extraordinary attitude stems from a number of factors. First, there is the simple fact that, for many men, making a woman pregnant is a proof of virility, and they are unable to think beyond that to the consequences. One recent study of male and female attitudes toward childbearing showed that men tend to view it as a kind of testament to their "immortality," rather than in terms of a personal relationship with a particular child, as women tend to do. . . . Men are more likely to take "principled" stands on moral issues without any regard for the human circumstances. Simone de Beauvoir notes that

> Men universally forbid abortion, but individually they accept

it as a convenient solution of a problem; they are able to contradict themselves with careless cynicism. . . .

Though feminism has never actually worked out a position on the role of men in abortion, in practice we have designated only one appropriate role for them, that of the "supportive man." In this scenario the man is to provide emotional support to a woman facing an unwanted pregnancy, and to help her carry out her choice, whatever it may be. In fostering this role we may give men the message, intentionally or not, that they should put aside whatever feelings or preferences they might have and just "be there" for the woman. Some progressive, "feminist" men, who are sympathetic to the goals of the women's movement and who in many cases actively work to support them, have particularly gravitated toward this role in their relationships with women. (A lot of other men are, of course, not so cooperative!) So, to a large extent, what we have encouraged in men is a passive, auxiliary role in abortion, allowing them to participate in a way that is helpful, but perhaps not, in some importance sense, truly meaningful. Perhaps this is just what we want. Abortion is, after all, a woman's choice. . . .

We have to acknowledge. . .that there is a grave inconsistency between our eagerness to involve men in all other aspects of reproduction and our unwillingness to allow them a similar role in abortion. This means we must acknowledge and validate men's role in the act of procreation. It really does take two. This isn't to suggest that men's and women's part in creating life are somehow equivalent, as some maintain. They obviously are not. Nature involves women in the reproductive process in a total physical and emotional way. We go through pregnancy, labour, birth, postpartum and breastfeeding, with all their attendant physical, hormonal and psychological changes. By contrast, nature does not even provide us with a sure way of verifying which man has fathered which child. But, if we are serious in our efforts to, in a sense, right nature's imbalance and make reproduction a truly joint effort, it behooves us to make more room for men in the abortion process, to allow them a meaningful role that acknowledges their part in procreation.

A Minefield of Problems

This stance poses, of course, a veritable minefield of problems, which we must traverse carefully if we are to maintain our hard-fought struggle for control over our bodies. The Right-to-Life movement has long argued for male involvement in abortion decisions—as long as the men involved are against abortion. On Father's Day, 1984, a group of anti-abortionists picketed a number of Toronto hospitals to dramatize their contention that men should have the right to veto abortions. Some of the participants interviewed used arguments that were uncomfortably close to the feminist view that reproduction should be a shared responsibility. Raising children "is not woman's work, it's humanity's work," said one man. We should have no illusions about the fact that our arguments for greater male involvement can and will be used against us. This does not mean that we should reject them altogether, but only that we must be continually clarifying and strengthening our position.

To many men, "meaningful involvement" equals control. The only power they know is power over others. They do not understand how to participate in truly cooperative decision-making. As a rule women are much more schooled in the art of cooperation, of sharing power and encouraging others to offer input, whether we agree with it or not. So when we call for greater male involvement in abortion and other reproductive matters, we must do so with the regrettable understanding that many men, perhaps most men, are not yet capable of this kind of powersharing, and we must act accordingly.

A Woman's Decision

We can say that we support male involvement in abortion decisions, but, as always, life presents us with complex, unwieldy situations where hard-and-fast rules can't be applied. For example, if the man withdraws from the relationship as soon as he finds out about the pregnancy, there is no question of his continued involvement in the process—he has made his choice. But what about women who don't tell their partners they are pregnant, who simply go off and quietly have an abortion? Are we dictating to them that they must involve their partners? Obviously we cannot do so. Most often when a woman does this, she has good reason to believe that telling her lover about the pregnancy may have bad repercussions. She may fear that he will try to prevent her from having the abortion, or may actually physically harm her. It is an uncomfortable fact that pregnancy is one of the situations in which wife battering is most likely to occur, and some men have been known to respond to the news of an unwanted pregnancy with rage and violence because they feel "tricked" or blame the woman.

In the end we must come back to our starting point: abortion is still a woman's right, a woman's choice. This means that when push comes to shove, when a man and a woman cannot come to agreement, it is the woman's wishes that must prevail. We cannot allow men any kind of absolute veto over our abortion decisions.

VIEWPOINT

5

"The right to choose to have an abortion is so personal and so essential . . . that without this right women cannot exercise other fundamental rights and liberties guaranteed by the Constitution."

Abortion Is a Constitutional Right

Lynn M. Paltrow

In 1985, the United States Justice Department under President Ronald Reagan filed a brief to return abortion laws to the states. If approved, the abortion law would return to its previous status before the *Roe v. Wade* decision, the 1973 landmark case that recognized abortion as a fundamental constitutional right and made abortion legal in all states. Many organizations also filed briefs along with Reagan's to either support or oppose his decision. The following viewpoint is excerpted from one of those briefs, written by Lynn M. Paltrow for the National Abortion Rights Action League, a pro-choice organization. In it, the author argues that without legal abortion women would be denied their constitutional rights of privacy and personal liberty.

As you read, consider the following questions:

1. According to the authors, which constitutional rights does legal abortion support?
2. The authors believe that imperfect contraceptives make it imperative that abortion remain legal. Do you agree?

"To 'Return the Law to the Condition' Before Roe Would Deny Women Their Fundamental Constitutional Rights" by Lynn M. Paltrow, published in an August 29, 1985 Amicus Curiae prepared and filed by the National Abortion Rights Action League. Reprinted with permission.

The Constitutional basis for *Roe v. Wade* is found in the personal liberty guaranteed by the Fourteenth Amendment, in the Bill of Rights and its penumbras, and is manifest in the stories of American women trying to lead meaningful, responsible, and caring lives. In *Roe v. Wade* [the Supreme] Court held that the "right of privacy . . . founded in the Fourteenth Amendment's concept of personal liberty and restrictions on state action . . . is broad enough to encompass a woman's decision whether or not to terminate her pregnancy." This decision stands on the long-recognized and essential element of personal liberty—an "individual's 'freedom of personal choice in matters of marriage and family life' . ". . . The right to choose to have an abortion is so personal and so essential to women's lives and well-being that without this right women cannot exercise other fundamental rights and liberties guaranteed by the Constitution.

The rights to privacy and personal liberty have been explicitly recognized to include the right to use contraceptives. Women are fertile from, approximately, the age of 15 to 45. Most women will spend the majority of these 30 years trying not to get pregnant. . . . But no contraceptives are one hundred percent safe and effective and they often fail despite conscientious use:

> I was a married woman using the birth control methods available at the time; a diaphram and a spermicide jelly. My first child was planned and I was very happy. Slightly more than two years later I had another planned child. Then I found myself pregnant with a child that would be only 17 months younger than the second child. I had used my birth control methods assiduously but to no avail. I accepted the fact of that child and loved it. Then I got pregnant again. This one would be only 13 months younger than the third child. I was faced with the unpleasant fact that I could not stop the babies from coming no matter what I did . . . . [The abortion] was a tremendous relief and I have never regretted it. My husband then had a vasectomy and our sex life was immensely improved. You cannot possibly know what it is like to be the helpless pawn of nature. I am a 71 year old widow . . . .

Abortion Is Necessary

Because contraceptives fail, and because they are not always available or possible to use, abortion is necessary if people are to be able to determine whether and when to "bear or beget a child." Individuals and couples choose the alternative of abortion so they can start or expand their families when they feel most ready and able to care for them. The following letters illustrate how important the right to choose to have an abortion is to those who are or intend to be parents:

> . . . We write together because abortion affects the lives of men and women . . . . Our decision was not a difficult one. It was not an agonizing one or a resolution of ambivalence.

In contrast our decision was a clear one. We were not ready to have a child. . . . Six years later our daughter, now almost three, was willfully conceived. It is difficult to adequately describe the difference between a wanted and an unwanted pregnancy. It is something like the difference between darkness and despair, and light and joy. We were ecstatic. The absolute joy we experience through our daughter comes in large part because we were ready to become parents. She has certainly been worth waiting for.

The right to choose to have an abortion is . . . an indispensable part of other liberty interests recognized by this Court.

This Court has stated that . . . .

> Without doubt [liberty] denotes not merely freedom from bodily restraint but also the right of the individual . . . to engage in any of the common occupations of life, to acquire useful knowledge, to marry, establish a home and bring up children, to worship God according to the dictates of his own conscience, and generally to enjoy those privileges long recognized by common law as essential to the orderly pursuit of happiness by free men.

Without the right to choose abortion the Fourteenth Amendment's guarantee of liberty has little meaning for women. With the right to choose abortion, women are able to enjoy, like men, the right to fully use the powers of their minds and bodies. . . .

Women choose to have an abortion because pregnancy and childbirth can prevent them from keeping their jobs, from feeding their families and from serving others in ways they consider necessary and appropriate . . . .

Pregnancy and childbirth may determine whether a woman ever gets to start or complete her education, which in turn will significantly influence her ability to support herself and her family. . . .

> I am a junior in college and am putting myself through because my father has been unemployed and my mother barely makes enough to support the rest of the family. I have promised to help put my brother through when I graduate next year and it's his turn. I was using a diaphragm for birth control but I got pregnant anyhow. There is no way I could continue this pregnancy because of my responsibilities to my family. I never wanted to be pregnant and if abortion were not legal I would do one on myself. . . .

An Unforced, Loving Marriage

Women choose to have an abortion because they want to wait until they can marry for sound, loving reasons:

> I had an abortion in 1949 because I could not go through with a loveless marriage for the sake of a child I did not want . . . . The benefits were incalculable. I was able to terminate the pregnancy, to complete my education, start a professional career, and, three years later marry a man I did love. We subsequently had three beautiful children by choice. . . .

The availability of abortion makes it possible for people not only to choose the number of children they want, but also to create the kind of family life they have envisioned for themselves, to meet their responsibilities to already existing family members, and to raise their children according to their values. . . .

> I am sole support of three children because my husband left three years ago with another woman. He does not pay child support and cannot be found to force him. I have a very hard time trying to do it myself. I just got a new job that pays better, but I still don't have benefits yet. If I have another baby I'll have to go back on welfare and I hate to do that because it does not set a good example for kids. . . .

The decision to have an abortion often reflects or is motivated by religious or spiritual beliefs that place priority on service and conduct of life as values even higher than procreation. . . .

Finally, if a woman cannot choose to terminate an unwanted pregnancy, she is denied the right to the "possession and control" of her own body. One of the most sacred rights of common law. . . .

> I was furiously angry, dismayed, dismal, by turns. I could not justify an abortion on economic grounds, on grounds of insufficient competence or on any other of a multitude of what might be perceived as "legitimate" reasons. But I kept being struck

by the ultimate unfairness of it all. I could not conceive of any event which would so profoundly impact upon any man. Surely my husband would experience some additional financial burden, and additional "fatherly" chores, but his whole future plan was not hostage to this unchosen, undesired event. Basically his life would remain the same progression of ordered events as before. . . .

Freedom to Decide

The freedom to decide whether or not to terminate a pregnancy is intimately connected to a woman's ability to be a full and equal participant in this society. Without the right to choose to have an abortion, women are not free to make and carry out fundamental, life-shaping decisions about work, education, marriage, family, home, health, and happiness. In short, without the right to choose to have an abortion, women are denied their constitutional rights of privacy and personal liberty.

Certain Rights Inalienable

Whether human life begins before birth is a matter of religious belief, and no group should be allowed to impose its views on those with different convictions. In a free and diverse society, people have different opinions on this question—as they do on the morality of marriage and divorce, how to raise their children, and dietary restrictions. A premise of our system from the beginning is that certain rights are not subject to political control. History convincingly shows the dangers when government power is used to coerce people on matters of conscience.

Norman Dorsen, *Los Angeles Times*, August 11, 1985.

Recognizing the profoundly personal nature of the abortion decision, this Court restricted government intrusion into the intimate relations of husbands and wives, into the family and into the hearts and minds of American women struggling to lead lives of integrity and dignity. This Court's decision in *Roe v. Wade* has dramatically improved the lives and health of American women and protected a right that is both fundamental and indispensable to women's ability to lead full and meaningful lives.

6 VIEWPOINT

"It is difficult to explain how a moral America . . . has the most permissive abortion law of any Western country, recognizing virtually no protection for unborn human beings."

Abortion Should Not Be a Constitutional Right

John Cardinal O'Connor

Opponents of legal abortion do not see it as a constitutional right. They argue that the law places many limits on people's freedom of choice, and should do so in the case of abortion. In fact, abortion foes see the law favoring one set of legal rights, the woman's, over another's, the unborn child's. John Cardinal O'Connor, the Roman Catholic Archbishop of New York and a staunch and outspoken opponent of abortion, agrees with these arguments. In the following viewpoint, he argues that abortion laws must change to protect the unborn.

As you read, consider the following questions:

1. What reasons does the author give to support his claim that laws should legislate morality?
2. The author makes a connection between abortion laws and child abuse and civil rights. What is his point?
3. After reading this viewpoint and the previous viewpoint, do you believe government should be involved in the abortion decision? Why or why not?

John Cardinal O'Connor, "Human Lives, Human Rights," *The Human Life Review*, Winter/Spring 1985. Reprinted with the author's permission.

Since 1973 some of the finest legal scholars in the United States have argued that the Supreme Court decisions were not solidly based on the Constitution, and one Supreme Court justice who dissented from the majority called the abortion decision an act of "raw judicial power." In other words, the will of seven justices was imposed on an entire nation.

Given this reality, when charges are so loosely made that those who plead for a recovery of legal protection for the unborn are trying to impose their will on the majority, it is apparently forgotten that virtually every state in the union had some kind of protective law which was swept away by the Supreme Court. If we are going to argue that law must reflect a consensus, we must admit that there was a strong, national consensus against abortion on demand before the Supreme Court issued its decree that the unborn is "not a person whose life state law could legally protect."

There are those who argue that we cannot legislate morality and that the answer to abortion does not lie in the law. The reality is that we do legislate behavior every day. Our entire society is structured by law. We legislate against going through red lights, selling heroin, committing murder, burning down peoples' houses, stealing, child abuse, slavery and a thousand other acts that would deprive other people of their rights.

And this is precisely the key: Law is intended to protect us from one another regardless of private and personal moral beliefs. The law does not ask me if I personally believe stealing to be moral or immoral. The law does not ask me if my religion encourages me to burn down houses. As far as the law is concerned, the distinction between private and public morality is quite clear. Basically, when I violate other people's rights, I am involved in a matter of public morality, subject to penalty under law.

Is it outlandish to think that laws against abortions might have some protective effect? It is obvious that law is not the entire answer to abortion. Nor is it the entire answer to theft, arson, child abuse or shooting police officers. Everybody knows that. But who would suggest that we repeal the laws against such crimes because the laws are so often broken? . . .

Why Laws Against Child Abuse?

Why maintain laws against child abuse when abortion—the most violent form of child abuse in society—is protected as a right? Why have laws against racism when—as the 10 black Roman Catholic bishops of the United States recently charged—liberal abortion policies amount to another form of subjugation of poor black people.

Deeply as we feel the pain of the individual and aware as we are that many, many women have abortions because that seems to them their only choice, we cannot, we must not, treat abortion as though it were a matter of concern only to an individual woman or man or family. We are already seeing cruel signs of what an abortion mentality can mean for all society.

Again we ask how safe will the retarded be, the handicapped, the aged, the wheelchaired, the incurably ill, when the so-called "quality of life" becomes the determinant of who is to live and who is to die? Who is to determine which life is "meaningful," which life is not? Who is to have a right to the world's resources, to food, to housing, to medical care? The prospects are frightening and far too realistic to be brushed aside as "scare tactics."

Reprinted by permission: Tribune Media Services.

Father [Theodore] Hesburgh of Notre Dame phrases the issue well. "It is difficult to explain how a moral America, so brilliantly successful in confronting racial injustice in the '60s, has the most permissive abortion law of any Western country, recognizing virtually no protection for unborn human beings."

So we must change the laws. This is one reason why I am encouraged by [New York] Gov. [Mario] Cuomo's calling for a task force to "take our highest aspirations and most noble pronouncements about life and seek to convert them into working laws and policies." . . . We continue to look to our highest elected officials for leadership in bringing about those changes in current laws and policies so critically needed to protect every human life at every stage of existence.

a critical thinking skill

Understanding Words in Context

Readers occasionally come across words which they do not recognize. And frequently, because they do not know a word or words, they will not fully understand the passage being read. Obviously, the reader can look up an unfamiliar word in a dictionary. However, by carefully examining the word in the context in which it is used, the word's meaning can often be determined. A careful reader may find clues to the meaning of the word in surrounding words, ideas, and attitudes.

Below are excerpts from the viewpoints in this chapter. In each excerpt, one or two words are printed in italics. Try to determine the meaning of each word by reading the excerpt. Under each excerpt you will find four definitions for the italicized word. Choose the one that is closest to your understanding of the word.

Finally, use a dictionary to see how well you have understood the words in context. It will be helpful to discuss with others the clues which helped you decide on each word's meaning.

1. The *MULTIFACETED* pressures generated by the women's movement in the last decade have gone well beyond the demand that women receive equal pay for equal work.

   MULTIFACETED means:

   a) many-sided
   b) great
   c) primary
   d) final

2. To defend the morality of *PROCREATIVE* choice for women is not to deny *REVERENCE* toward or appreciation for many women's deep commitment to childbearing and child nurturance.

   PROCREATIVE means:

   a) creative
   b) work
   c) reproductive
   d) equal

   REVERENCE means:

   a) contempt
   b) respect
   c) religious feeling
   d) hatred

3. We drag children into *AD HOC* alternative families with shifting memberships.

   AD HOC means:
   a) planned c) destructive
   b) arranged d) unprepared

4. Pro-abortionists argue that women do agonize over the abortion decision and so do consider the moral issues involved. This argument that many women anguish over their choice still *DEFERS* to *OBSOLESCENT*, unused values.

   DEFERS means:
   a) surrenders c) suggests
   b) battles d) argues

   OBSOLESCENT means:
   a) current c) popular
   b) unfashionable d) moral

5. Legal abortion is an *INDISPENSABLE* part of women's freedom. It has helped women gain an equal footing in the workplace and to plan their lives without the fear of unwanted pregnancy.

   INDISPENSABLE means:
   a) unnecessary c) essential
   b) unbelievable d) restrictive

6. Feminists have gone a long way toward *ERADICATING* the sexist notion that an unwanted pregnancy is the fault of the woman.

   ERADICATING means:
   a) believing c) promoting
   b) popularizing d) eliminating

7. Evidence over the centuries has shown women that it is *PRUDENT* to not involve men in the abortion decision.

   PRUDENT means:
   a) wise c) petty
   b) stupid d) necessary

8. Often men take the opposite *TACK* when confronted with an abortion.

   TACK means:
   a) point c) belief
   b) a method of action d) idea

Periodical Bibliography

The following list of periodical articles deals with the subject matter of this chapter.

Burke J. Balch	"Mixing Personal Morality and Public Policy," *The New York Times*, September 20, 1984.
Christianity and Crisis	"Women, Abortion, and Autonomy," March 5, 1984.
Christianity and Crisis	"Abortion: Why Don't We All Get Smart?" April 15, 1985.
Dudley Clendinen	"The Abortion Conflict: What It Does to One Doctor," *The New York Times Magazine*, August 11, 1985.
Daughters of Sarah	Special issue on abortion, September/ October 1985.
Bob Hutchinson	"A Choice Convert to the Prolife Cause," *SALT*, May 1985.
John D. Lofton	"Pro-Choicer Hoist By Her Own Petard," *Manchester Union Leader*, May 16, 1985.
Patricia O'Brien	"Man's Feelings Forgotten in Decisions on Abortion," *St. Paul Sunday Pioneer Press*, October 16, 1983.
Katha Pollitt	"Hentoff, Are You Listening?" *Mother Jones*, February/March 1985.
Joseph Sobran	"Playing Their Motherhood Card," *National Right to Life News*, June 20, 1985. Available from 419 Seventh St., NW, Suite 402, Washington, DC 20005.
John E. Swomley	"Politics Centered Upon Abortion," *The Churchman*, April 1985.
The Wanderer	"On Being 'Personally Opposed' to the 'Final Solution,' " November 22, 1984. Available from 201 Ohio St., St. Paul, MN 55101.
Anne Wilson	"The Abortion Decision Is Rarely Easy," *Engage/Social Action*, March 1983.

Is Abortion Immoral?

1 VIEWPOINT

"[The pro-abortion groups] continue to urge women to climb toward what is viewed as their rights over the bodies of 17 million aborted children."

Abortion Is Immoral

Vernie Dale

For many, the central issue in the abortion debate focuses on one question: is abortion the taking of a human life? Many people who believe it is insist that abortion can never be a moral choice. In the following viewpoint, Vernie Dale argues that abortion cannot merely be a woman's right. It is always wrong, she argues, and defeats woman's personal, political and biological natures. Ms. Dale is the author of *When a Wife Turns Forty* and works at a pregnancy clinic.

As you read, consider the following questions:

1. Why does the author believe the tide is turning against women's liberation?
2. How are women encouraged to think of themselves as victims by the women's movement, according to the author?
3. Why does the author believe the abortion mentality weakens women?

Vernie Dale, "Pro-Choice Activists Are Aborting Women's Liberation," *National Catholic Reporter*, February 22, 1985. Reprinted by permission of the National Catholic Reporter, PO Box 281, Kansas City, MO 64141 and the author.

The tide is turning against proponents of abortion and the reason has little to do with politics or rhetoric. The tide is turning because more and more people recognize the biggest anchor dragging at the women's movement, the group doing the most to ensure women won't be taken seriously as responsible and mature determiners of their own destiny, are abortion activists. Because such activism does not serve the growth of women, it has clashed head-on with the forces of true liberation, and is going under. This is true for several reasons.

First, the controversy over abortion has obscured the real issue facing today's woman—her need to grow beyond stereotypes, beyond submission, and into assertive wholeness. Whenever an individual or a group awakens to the fact it has been treated unjustly, the first reaction is anger. This emotion is good, and part of the maturation process, but very often the anger is first expressed as aggression. Persons outgrowing submissive behavior have so much stored-up bitterness, such memories of powerlessness and so little knowledge of how to make themselves heard, that violence toward others is the result. A tremendous outpouring of decades of repressed anger does terrible damage, as we saw in the race riots of the 1960s; yet this emotional discharge can clear the way for logic, compassion and a more effective response to discrimination, as in the candidacy of Jesse Jackson. Aggression, therefore, is often one of the way stations toward true assertion—the clear expression of one's needs while taking responsibility for one's behavior.

It's Time to Move On

The women's movement, too, has been caught up in this same process—awakening, anger, aggression, assertion. But the pro-abortion groups have not encouraged women to move beyond the aggressive stage. They continue to urge women to climb toward what is viewed as their rights over the bodies of 17 million aborted children. American men and women are among the most fair-minded on earth, but more and more of us have begun to feel 1.5 *million* abortions a year, 4,000 a day, are enough. It is time to move on. Women have grown beyond aggression.

Second, the abortion mentality has encouraged women to think of themselves as victims. Much emphasis, for example, is placed on pregnancy as a result of rape, even though the statistics show only about .1 per cent of all rapes actually result in conception. That means the vast majority of pregnancies that ended in abortion were the result of some modicum of choice. Yet abortion advocates ignore the confusion, pain and despair that are often involved in this choice and zero in on the problem after pregnancy has already occurred. The underlying assumption is that a woman does not have, and is not expected to have, any control over her own body until *after* a male partner is finished with it. Only then does she hear talk of "rights." No emphasis is placed on the *before*, on developing her ability to assert herself before an unwanted pregnancy occurs. No emphasis is placed on developing a woman's power to make it on her own, without having to please a man, or having to bind one to herself through pregnancy. Women have great control over their own lives, great ability for rational and assertive decision-making, but many need to be educated to this fact, need to know how to develop such self-assertion and self-esteem. People who urge abortion as the solution to unwanted pregnancies are merely touching up the x-rays of a far deeper hurt. Women need to be encouraged to summon up their own inner strengths, their own inner healing, to throw off the cloak of masochistic victimhood and develop their own power to choose.

Simplistic Attitude

Yet pro-abortion rhetoric discourages this because it discourages the development of the thinking function in women. Because of the way they were raised, many women respond to their perceptions of reality with their emotions. This is good, and sorely needed by the world, but in order to grow women must also develop their powers of rational thought. Otherwise they will constantly be in danger of manipulation by those who arouse their emotions of anger and the sense of injustice through catchwords and cliches. The term "pro-choice," for example, evokes their sense of fairness. But women are going further and considering what is actually be-

Bill DeOre, *The Dallas Morning News*, reprinted with permission.

ing chosen—the killing of an innocent human life. Another phrase is "a woman's right over her own body"—an idea that more and more women are realizing ignores the unborn child's right to *his* or *her* body. Other women have seen that such a phrase glosses over the responsibility of men and women for using their bodies in a way which produces results not really wanted or intended.

The abortion mentality has arisen from, and tends to promote, the very patriarchal thinking the women's movement is struggling to change. The immature masculine reaction to any problem is usually denial of some kind, a projection of the problem onto others, or violence. This mentality sees nuclear war as the way to deal with enemies, rape as the way to deal with uppity women and abortion as the way to "solve" the problem of an unwanted pregnancy. Such violent behavior never looks within, never asks, "How have I contributed to this problem and what responsibility do I have to prevent its recurrence?" It is highly emotional in nature, sees the other as the source of every problem and is bent on destruction and elimination. Many proabortionists are highly sensitive to the notion they may be subtly dependent on men, stating they will never allow male church or government leaders to dictate to them what they can do with their own bodies. Yet these same groups advocate the funding of a multimillion-dollar abortion industry run almost exclusively by men, and allow men to escape all responsibility for the children they have helped create.

"Easy, Quick and Confidential"

Women have worked long and hard to change the patronizing attitude which assumes any man can easily and quickly solve all a woman's problems. "Here's the money; go get an abortion." It's all perfectly legal, and a woman's *right*. By accepting this view of things, women buy into the trivializing of relationships and the cheapening of sexuality. Completely ignored is humankind's deep need for love, its longing for an end to loneliness. Many men would rather not look at these things; it is up to the women's movement to insist they do, and not join with them in sweeping everything under the rug. "Easy, quick and confidential" say the abortion ads—just as a male-dominated society would like it to be.

Finally, women are abandoning the abortion mentality because it weakens their great strengths: creation, compassion and the ability to look beneath the surface appearance of things. Women are led to denigrate their creative ability to form a human being, to be the eucharistic presence that says to the child within, "This is my body; it is for you." The beautiful pre-born child, delicate as a seashell, is relegated to the status of "product of pregnancy" and never seen as the miracle only a woman can perform.

Women are urged to believe the child within her can feel no pain, has no personality, is not even human. Compassion for the small and dependent is drowned under a demand for "rights," for quick solutions, for more affluent life-styles; and suddenly women find themselves acting just like men, like the men responsible for wars and reprisals and holocausts espousing the violent way out, denying the humanity of the ones to be destroyed, killing whoever stands in the way.

The tide is turning against abortion advocates because women have grown to a far greater stature. They are looking at responsibilities as well as rights, at choosing instead of reacting, at nourishing compassion rather than fear. More and more they are taking up prophetic roles as protectors of the least of the little ones, as witnesses to the beauty and innocence which constantly redeem even the worst of our mistakes.

VIEWPOINT 2

"Women themselves will finally achieve full personhood . . . when we have the right, unquestioned and unabrogated, to choose not to be pregnant."

Abortion Is Not Immoral

Barbara Ehrenreich

Barbara Ehrenreich is a contributing editor to *Ms.* magazine, the author of *The Hearts of Men: American Dreams and the Flight from Commitment*, and a contributor to periodicals and newspapers. In the following viewpoint, Ms. Ehrenreich argues that abortion would be neither a "vexing moral dilemma" nor a question of murder if people stopped framing the abortion issue in moral terms. Abortion should instead be viewed as a sometimes necessary choice a woman must make in order to be in charge of her life.

As you read, consider the following questions:

1. Ms. Ehrenreich claims to have only one regret about her abortions. What is it? What do you think of this?
2. How does the author describe a pregnant person? What do you think about her description?
3. How does society encourage abortion, according to the author?

Quite apart from blowing up clinics and terrorizing patients, the antiabortion movement can take credit for a more subtle and lasting kind of damage: It has succeeded in getting even pro-choice people to think of abortion as a "moral dilemma," an "agonizing decision" and related code phrases for something murky and compromising, like the traffic in infant formula mix. In liberal circles, it has become unstylish to discuss abortion without using words like "complex," "painful" and the rest of the mealy-mouthed vocabulary of evasion. Regrets are also fashionable, and one otherwise feminist author writes recently of mourning, each year following her abortion, the putative birthday of her discarded fetus.

I cannot speak for other women, of course, but the one regret I have about my own abortions is that they cost money that might otherwise have been spent on something more pleasurable, like taking the kids to movies and theme parks. Yes, that is abortions, plural (two in my case)—a possibility that is not confined to the promiscuous, the disorderly or the ignorant. In fact, my credentials for dealing with the technology of contraception are first rate: I have a Ph.D. in biology that is now a bit obsolescent but still good for conjuring up vivid mental pictures of zygotes and ova, and I was actually paid, at one point in my life, to teach other women about the mysteries of reproductive biology.

Contraception Unreliable

Yet, as every party to the abortion debate should know, those methods of contraception that are truly safe are not absolutely reliable no matter how reliably they are used. Many women, like myself, have felt free to choose the safest methods because legal abortion is available as a backup to contraception. Anyone who finds that a thoughtless, immoral choice should speak to the orphans of women whose wombs were perforated by Dalkon shields or whose strokes were brought on by high-estrogen birth-control pills.

I refer you to the orphans only because it no longer seems to be good form to mention women themselves in discussions of abortion. In most of the antiabortion literature I have seen, women are so invisible that an uninformed reader might conclude that fetuses reside in artificially warm tissue culture flasks or similar containers. It must be enormously difficult for the antiabortionist to face up to the fact that real fetuses can only survive inside women, who, unlike any kind of laboratory apparatus, have thoughts, feelings, aspirations, responsibilities and, very often, checkbooks. Anyone who thinks for a moment about women's role in reproductive biology could never blithely recommend "adoption, not abortion," because women have to go through something unknown to fetuses or men, and that is pregnancy.

From the point of view of a fetus, pregnancy is no doubt a good deal. But consider it for a moment from the point of view of the pregnant person (if ''woman'' is too incendiary and feminist a term) and without reference to its potential issue. We are talking about a nine-month bout of symptoms of varying severity, often including nausea, skin discolorations, extreme bloating and swelling, insomnia, narcolepsy, hair loss, varicose veins, hemorrhoids, indigestion and irreversible weight gain, and culminating in a physiological crisis which is occasionally fatal and almost always excruciatingly painful. If men were equally at risk for this condition—if they knew that their bellies might swell as if they were suffering from end-stage cirrhosis, that they would have to go for nearly a year without a stiff drink, a cigarette or even an aspirin, that they would be subject to fainting spells and unable to fight their way onto commuter trains—then I am sure that pregnancy would be classified as a sexually transmitted disease and abortions would be no more controversial than emergency appendectomies.

Abortion Aids Women

We know that for the very young abortion may mean the difference between continuing school or dropping out. It may mean the difference between welfare and self-sufficiency. It may mean not having to suffer the pain of giving a child away. Abortion will allow others to pursue careers or prevent forced marriages. It can make the difference between adequate and inadequate nutrition, clothing, and shelter. For some it will mean not having to bear a rapist's or relative's baby. It can preserve the physical health and sometimes the lives of women who have chronic illness or disease. It can preserve the mental health of those hovering on the brink of breakdowns. It can prevent the birth of children doomed to die.

Carole Dornblasser and Uta Landy, *The Abortion Guide*, 1982.

Adding babies to the picture does not make it all that much prettier, even if you are, as I am, a fool for short, dimpled people with drool on their chins. For no matter how charming the outcome of pregnancy that is allowed to go to term no one is likely to come forth and offer to finance its Pampers or pay its college tuition. Nor are the opponents of abortion promising a guaranteed annual income, subsidized housing, national health insurance and other measures that might take some of the terror out of parenthood. We all seem to expect the individual parents to shoulder the entire burden of supporting any offspring that can be traced to them, and, in the all-too-common event that the father cannot be identified or has skipped town to avoid child-support payments, ''parent'' means mother.

When society does step in to help out a poor woman attempting to raise children on her own, all that it customarily has to offer is some government-surplus cheese, a monthly allowance so small it would barely keep a yuppie male in running shoes, and the contemptuous epithet "welfare cheat." It would be far more reasonable to honor the survivors of pregnancy in childbirth with at least the same respect and special benefits that we give, without a second thought, to veterans of foreign wars.

But, you will object, I have greatly exaggerated the discomforts of pregnancy and the hazards of childbearing, which many women undergo quite cheerfully. This is true, at least to an extent. In my own case, the case of my planned and wanted pregnancies, I managed to interpret morning sickness as a sign of fetus tenacity and to find, in the hypertrophy of my belly, a voluptuousness ordinarily unknown to the skinny. But this only proves my point: A society that is able to make a good thing out of pregnancy is certainly free to choose how to regard abortion. We can treat it as a necessary adjunct to contraception, or as a vexing moral dilemma, or as a form of homicide—and whichever we choose, that is how we will tend to experience it.

"Baby Killer"

So I will admit that I might not have been so calm and determined about my abortions if I had had to cross a picket line of earnest people yelling "baby killer," or if I felt that I might be blown to bits in the middle of a vacuum aspiration. Conversely, though, we would be hearing a lot less about ambivalence and regrets if there were not so much liberal head-scratching going on. Abortions will surely continue, as they have through human history, whether we approve or disapprove or hem and haw. The question that worries me is: How is, say, a 16-year-old girl going to feel after an abortion? Like a convicted sex offender, a murderess on parole? Or like a young woman who is capable, as the guidance counselors say, of taking charge of her life?

This is our choice, for biology will never have an answer to that strange and cabalistic question of when a fetus becomes a person. Potential persons are lost every day as a result of miscarriage, contraception or someone's simple failure to respond to a friendly wink. What we can answer, with a minimum of throat-clearing and moral agonizing, is the question of when women themselves will finally achieve full personhood: And that is when we have the right, unquestioned and unabrogated, to *choose* not to be pregnant when we decide not to be pregnant.

3 VIEWPOINT

"Why can we not view abortion as one of those anguished decisions in which human beings struggle to do the best they can in trying circumstances?"

Morality Oversimplifies the Abortion Decision

Rachel Richardson Smith

In the midst of the abortion controversy are people who disagree with the tactics and attitudes of pro-life groups yet do not favor abortion. In the following viewpoint, Rachel Richardson Smith advocates this view. A mother and theology student in North Carolina, Ms. Smith is both anti-abortion and pro-choice. She doesn't want anyone to be trapped by an unwanted pregnancy, yet she believes abortion is the taking of a human life, an idea that keeps her from wholeheartedly embracing the pro-choice camp. Ms. Smith believes that while pro-lifers would like to enforce their narrow morality, pro-choicers refuse to acknowledge that abortion is not the perfect answer. What is needed, she believes, is an acknowledgment by both groups that the abortion decision cannot be defined in simple moral terms.

As you read, consider the following questions:

1. The author states why she cannot side with the pro-choice people nor the pro-abortion people. What reasons does she give?
2. How does having given birth and being a mother influence the author's views?

I cannot bring myself to say I am in favor of abortion. I don't want anyone to have one. I want people to use contraceptives and for those contraceptives to be foolproof. I want people to be responsible for their actions; mature in their decisions. I want children to be loved, wanted, well cared for.

I cannot bring myself to say I am against choice. I want women who are young, poor, single or all three to be able to direct the course of their lives. I want women who have had all the children they want or can afford or their bodies can withstand to be able to decide their future. I want women who are in bad marriages or destructive relationships to avoid being trapped by pregnancy.

So in these days when thousands rally in opposition to legalized abortion, when facilities providing abortions are bombed, when the president speaks glowingly of the growing momentum behind the anti-abortion movement, I find myself increasingly alienated from the pro-life groups.

At the same time, I am overwhelmed with mail from pro-choice groups. They, too, are mobilizing their forces, growing articulate in support of their cause, and they want my support. I am not sure I can give it.

A Member of Neither Camp

I find myself in the awkward position of being both anti-abortion and pro-choice. Neither group seems to be completely right—or wrong. It is not that I think abortion is wrong for me but acceptable for someone else. The question is far more complex than that.

Part of my problem is that what I think and how I feel about this issue are two entirely different matters. I know that unwanted children are often neglected, even abandoned. I know that many of those seeking abortions are children themselves. I know that making abortion illegal will not stop all women from having them.

I also know from experience the crisis an unplanned pregnancy can cause. Yet I have felt the joy of giving birth, the delight that comes from feeling a baby's skin against my own. I know how hard it is to parent a child and how deeply satisfying it can be. My children sometimes provoke me and cause me endless frustration, but I can still look at them with tenderness and wonder at the miracle of it all. The lessons of my own experience produce conflicting emotions. Theory collides with reality.

It concerns me that both groups present themselves in absolutes. They are committed and they want me to commit. They do not recognize the gray area where I seem to be languishing. Each group has the right answer—the only answer.

Pro-Life Tactics

Yet I am uncomfortable in either camp. I have nothing in common with pro-lifers. I am horrified by their scare tactics, their pictures of well-formed fetuses tossed in a metal pan, their cruel slogans. I cannot condone their flagrant misuse of Scripture and unforgiving spirit. There is a meanness about their position that causes them to pass judgment on the lives of women in a way I could never do.

A Confusing Issue

I don't believe in the absolute moral rights of the unborn nor that their legal rights outweigh those of the women who carry them. Yet, I see grave dangers to the impaired and old in any kind of "whose life is worth more" judgment. . . .

Yet I, who have borne five children and would never have considered abortion for myself, would not go back to those days when women determined to have abortions had to search desperately and illegally or resorted to dangerous and dirty methods. . . .

Unless we can find and humbly love one another on that dangerous ground labeled "unsure on this one," we are destroyed.

Joan Turner Beifuss, *The National Catholic Reporter*, February 8, 1985.

The pro-life groups, with their fundamentalist religious attitudes, have a fear and an abhorrence of sex, especially premarital sex. In their view abortion only compounds the sexual sin. What I find incomprehensible is that even as they are opposed to abortion they are also opposed to alternative solutions. They are squeamish about sex education in schools. They don't want teens to have contraceptives without parental consent. They offer little aid or sympathy to unwed mothers. They are the vigilant guardians of a narrow morality.

I wonder how abortion got to be the greatest of all sins? What about poverty, ignorance, hunger, weaponry?

The only thing the anti-abortion groups seem to have right is that abortion is indeed the taking of human life. I simply cannot escape this one glaring fact. Call it what you will—fertilized egg, embryo, fetus. What we have here is human life. If it were just a mass of tissue there would be no debate. So I agree that abortion ends a life. But the anti-abortionists are wrong to call it murder.

Homicide Sometimes Acceptable

The sad truth is that homicide is not always against the law. Our society does not categorically recognize the sanctity of human life. There are a number of legal and apparently socially acceptable ways to take human life. "Justifiable" homicide includes the death penalty, war, killing in self-defense. It seems to me that as a society we need to come to grips with our own ambiguity concerning the value of human life. If we are to value and protect unborn life so stringently, why do we not also value and protect life already born?

Why can't we see abortion for the human tragedy it is? No woman plans for her life to turn out that way. Even the most effective contraceptives are no guarantee against pregnancy. Loneliness, ignorance, immaturity can lead to decisions (or lack of decisions) that may result in untimely pregnancy. People make mistakes.

What many people seem to misunderstand is that no woman wants to have an abortion. Circumstances demand it; women do it. No woman reacts to abortion with joy. Relief, yes. But also ambivalence, grief, despair, guilt.

Not the Perfect Answer

The pro-choice groups do not seem to acknowledge that abortion is not a perfect answer. What goes unsaid is that when a woman has an abortion she loses more than an unwanted pregnancy. Often she loses her self-respect. No woman can forget a pregnancy no matter how it ends.

Why can we not view abortion as one of those anguished decisions in which human beings struggle to do the best they can in trying circumstances? Why is abortion viewed so coldly and factually on the one hand and so judgmentally on the other? Why is it not akin to the same painful experience families must sometimes make to allow a loved one to die?

I wonder how we can begin to change the context in which we think about abortion. How can we begin to think about it redemptively? What is it in the trauma of loss of life—be it loved or unloved, born or unborn—from which we can learn? There is much I have yet to resolve. Even as I refuse to pass judgment on other women's lives, I weep for the children who might have been. I suspect I am not alone.

4 VIEWPOINT

"Abortion is not an issue of private morality. Pro-life people perceive themselves involved in the humane and progressive struggle . . . for the rights of those who are weak and voiceless."

The Religious Argument Against Abortion

Francis X. Meehan

While it would be possible to compile an anthology dealing with the issue of abortion without presenting the religious arguments for and against, it would not accurately portray the overall abortion debate. Many people with similar religious views disagree on the morality of abortion. In the following viewpoint, Francis X. Meehan argues that abortion is a moral and religious issue and should not be allowed to continue on these grounds. Father Meehan is an instructor in Moral Theology at St. Charles Borromeo Seminary in the Archdiocese of Philadelphia.

As you read, consider the following questions:

1. The author rejects the argument that men cannot have a say in the abortion decision. Why does he believe it to be an irrelevant issue?
2. Should the law legislate morality, according to the author? Why or why not?

Excerpts from "Pro-Life Work and Social Justice" by Francis X. Meehan, first appeared in *Respect Life! 1979-80*, published by the United States Catholic Conference, Washington, DC and are used with permission.

When all is said and done, a theology for pro-life work need not be in any way complicated. The very first and last reason for respecting life is that the life *is there*. God's creation *is there*. And if God's creation is there, there is a deep and yet simple theology that knows that the Lord Jesus is present. He in whom all creation is summed up is found in every suffering or oppressed person. No theology can capture the depth and yet the simplicity of the Lord's theology: "I was hungry and you gave me food. . . .I assure you, as often as you did it for one of my least brothers, you did it for me" (Mt. 25:36-40). Let us begin our questions and answers knowing that all is summed up in this Word of the Lord.

Why should any minority be allowed to impose its view of the morality of abortion on the rest of the country?

This question comes up frequently. It carries false assumptions and oversimplifies socio-legal realities.

First, those who are against the present situation of abortion in this country may not be a minority. Sociological analysis indicates that much depends on how the question is asked. There are good grounds for thinking that those who favor the present fact of abortion on demand are the real minority, and that it is they who have imposed their morality on the rest of us—not to mention what they have imposed on several million children in the womb.

Second, even if those against abortion were a minority that would not settle the issue. It did not settle the issue of slavery or of discrimination. Abortion is not an issue of private morality. Pro-life people perceive themselves (rightly, I believe) involved in the humane and progressive struggle in this country for the rights of those who are weak and voiceless. This kind of social struggle cannot accept mere head-counting as a norm for who should have human rights.

Men and Abortion

How can a man dare to speak so easily on abortion? He has never been in the crucible of conflict which a woman may experience when she finds herself pregnant.

Simone Weil pointed out that it is a sign of spiritual maturity to know that two things diametrically opposed can both be true. I would like to make the same point—a little out of context, but not completely without context. A man cannot dare to speak about abortion. A man must dare to speak about abortion. Both are true. Abortion is a woman's issue. But abortion is a human issue.

There is a pastoral compassion that dares not judge the heart, but this cannot preclude all moral analysis. In the end, abortion is more than a personal moral dilemma. It is also a social phenomenon. Supreme Court rulings on abortion since 1973 have treated pregnancy as so exclusively the woman's concern that not even the father of the unborn child or parents of an unmarried minor considering abortion have any rights in the matter. This concept of pregnancy as the woman's private affair is an anthropological first in the history of cultures and civilizations.

The Church's judgment on abortion is neither male nor female. It is social. It places the rights of the child in the womb in that line of progressive social thought that sees individual dignity as inalienable. This is clearly an area where the Church has

There are those whom we do not hear, since they cannot speak for themselves. Justice and morality cry out that we must speak for them. No one else will.

Nackey Loeb for *The Union Leader*, reprinted with permission.

courageously allowed her *anima* to shine through—to use a Jungian term. It is in the end a pro-woman posture, which recognizes that she who was once treated as property must not undergo a double jeopardy. It is a Christian call to woman, who has been oppressed, to resist the easy tendency to become the new oppressor. . . .

Legislating Morality

Why legislate morality? Should church people and church groups be getting into political and legal matters like this?

The relationship between morality and law, as between Church and society, is surely complex. But in the practical world one must unravel complexity in the best way possible and then take a position. While the question raised here is certainly legitimate in itself, it is nevertheless often raised in a context that reveals individualistic and privatist assumptions.

In this country, which has been said to possess the "soul of a church," legal structures have a special power to teach and propagate morality—or immorality, as the case may be. People here and everywhere have a tendency to accept what is *given*. Hannah Arendt, the Jewish political philosopher, saw how this happened in Germany. She called it the "banality of evil." Things which a short time earlier would have been perceived as outrageous became acceptable, simply because a legal structure legitimized them. (The analogy is to be applied carefully. In no way do I imply that my adversaries are equivalent to Nazis.) I am saying that analysis of the impetus which social structure gives to a particular view of morality is highly relevant to abortion in this country.

Twenty years ago, most people and groups in this country would have been appalled had someone told them that the law would some day approve abortion on demand. Now many accept this state of affairs lock, stock, and barrel.

Legal structures, if they are not good ones, have a way of making it hard "for a good person to be good"—as the bishops of Appalachia put it. If, therefore, the Catholic Church or any church is serious about moral persuasion, concerned not only about private morality but about history itself and its impact on the human, there is no way for it to avoid becoming involved in structural issues, including issues of law and policy. It would be convenient for religion if there were some neutral, Olympian heights where it could preach pure doctrine in the abstract. But as far as abortion is concerned, there is little or no room for legal or political neutrality. Not to take a stand is ultimately to take a stand—in favor of the status quo.

5 VIEWPOINT

"Abortion is always tragic, but the tragedy of abortion is not always immoral."

Religious People Can Disagree on Abortion

Daniel C. Maguire

Daniel C. Maguire is professor of moral theology at Marquette University in Milwaukee, Wisconsin, and past president of the Society of Christian Ethics. Mr. Maguire has been and continues to be in the forefront of the abortion debate. Raising the ire of many of his colleagues of theology, and yet admired by those who support him in his position, Maguire continually attempts to straddle a delicate position: that of a religious person who supports an individual's right to decide whether or not to have an abortion. In the following viewpoint, he argues that the church has traditionally encouraged debate over a number of theological and moral issues. Church members' conflicting views over abortion should also be tolerated by the church, rather than singlemindedly condemning those who support abortion as immoral.

As you read, consider the following questions:

1. Why does the author believe there is so little debate in the church on the abortion issue?
2. Does the Bible forbid abortion, according to the author?
3. Should men have a right to deny women abortion, according to the author? Why or why not?

There are far more than five or six Catholic theologians today who approve abortions under a range of circumstances, and there are many spiritual and good people who find "cogent," non-frivolous reasons to disagree with the hierarchy's absolutism on this issue. This makes their disagreement a "solidly probable" and thoroughly respectable Catholic viewpoint. Abortion is always tragic, but the tragedy of abortion is not always immoral.

The Bible does not forbid abortion. Rather, the prohibition came from theological and biological views that were seriously deficient in a number of ways and that have been largely abandoned. . . .

Male Authority in the Church

Why has all authority on this issue been assumed by men who have not been assigned by biology to bear children or by history to rear them? Are the Catholic women who disagree with the bishops all weak-minded or evil? Is it possible that not a single Catholic bishop can see any ambiguity in any abortion decision?. . .

Since the so-called "prolife" movement is not dominated by vegetarian pacifists who find even nonpersonal life sacred, is the "prolife" fetal fixation innocent? Does it not make the fertilized egg the legal and moral peer of a woman? Indeed, in the moral calculus of those who oppose all abortion, does not the *potential* person outweigh the *actual* person of the woman? Why is the intense concern over the 1.5 million abortions not matched by an equal concern over the male-related causes of these 1.5 million unwanted pregnancies? Has the abortion ban been miraculously immune to the sexism rife in Christian history?

Feminist scholars have documented the long record of men's efforts to control the sexuality and reproductivity of women. Laws showcase our biases. Is there no sexist bias in the new Catholic Code of Canon Law? Is that code *for* life or *against* women's control of their reproductivity? After all, canon law excommunicates a person for aborting a fertilized egg, but not for killing a baby after birth. One senses here an agenda other than the simple concern for life.

What obsessions are operating? A person could push the nuclear button and blow the ozone lid off the earth or assassinate the president (but not the pope) without being excommunicated. But aborting a five-week-old precerebrate, prepersonal fetus would excommunicate him or her. May we uncritically allow such an embarrassing position to posture as "prolife"? Does it not assume that women cannot be trusted to make honorable decisions, and that only male-made laws and male-controlled funding can make women responsible and moral about their reproductivity?

The moral dilemma of choosing whether to have an abortion faces only some women between their teens and their 40s. The self-styled "prolife" movement is made up mainly of men and postfertile women. Is there nothing suspicious about passionately locating one's orthodoxy in an area where one will never be personally challenged or inconvenienced?

Illegal Abortion Would Be Wrong

Prohibition was wrong because it attempted to impose a private moral position on a pluralistic society. The prohibition of abortion is wrong for the same reason. Society must allow for the debate of valid issues, and then for freedom of choice, not coercion. Some moral positions are not within the pale of respectability, and we properly use coercion to prohibit them. Refusing to educate children, denying sick children blood transfusions, keeping snakes in a church for faith-testing are not respectable options, and we should forbid them. But most abortions are not in that category. Abortion is an issue deserving respectable debate.

A moral opinion merits respectable debate if it is supported by serious reasons which commend themselves to many people and if it has been endorsed by a number of reputable religious or other

humanitarian bodies. Note the two requirements: *good reasons* and *reliable authorities*. The principle of respectable debate is based on some confidence in the capacity of free minds to come to the truth, and on a distrust of authoritarian shortcuts to consensus and uniformity. This principle is integral to American political thought and to the Catholic doctrine of probabilism. On the other hand, prohibition represents a despairing effort to compel those whom one cannot convince; it can only raise new and unnecessary doubts about Catholic compatibility with democratic political life.

But what of legislators who personally believe that all abortion is wrong? Those legislators must recognize that it is not their function to impose their own private moral beliefs on a pluralistic society. St. Augustine and St. Thomas Aquinas both found prostitution morally repugnant, but felt that it should be legalized for the greater good of the society. St. Thomas wryly but wisely suggested that a good legislator should imitate God, who could eliminate certain evils but does not do so for the sake of the greater good. The greater good supported by the principle of respectable debate is the good of a free society where conscience is not unduly constrained on complex matters where good persons disagree. Thus a Catholic legislator who judges all abortions to be immoral may in good conscience support the decisions of *Roe v. Wade,* since that ruling is permissive rather than coercive. It forces no one to have an abortion, while it respects the moral freedom of those who judge some abortions to be moral.

Government Supports Essential Freedoms

Good government insists that essential freedoms be denied to no one. Essential freedoms concern basic goods such as the right to marry, the right to a trial by jury, the right to vote, the right to some education and the right to bear *or not to bear* children. The right not to bear children includes abortion as a means of last resort. Concerning such goods, government should not act to limit freedom along income lines, and should ensure that poverty takes no essential freedoms from any citizen. Furthermore, the denial of abortion funding to poor women is not a neutral stance, but a natalist one. The government takes sides on the abortion debate by continuing to pay for births while denying poor women funds for the abortion alternative that is available to the rich. Funding cutbacks are also forcing many to have later abortions, since they have to spend some months scraping up the funds denied them by the government. The denial of funding is an elitist denial of moral freedom to the poor and a stimulus for later or unsafe abortions.

a critical thinking skill

Recognizing Statements That Are Provable

From various sources of information we are constantly confronted with statements and generalizations about social and moral problems. In order to think clearly about these problems, it is useful to be able to make a basic distinction between statements for which evidence can be found and other statements which cannot be verified or proved because evidence is not available or the issue is too controversial.

Readers should constantly be aware that magazines, newspapers and other sources often contain statements of a controversial or questionable nature. The following activity is designed to allow experimentation with statements that are provable and those that are not.

Most of the following statements are taken from the viewpoints in this chapter. Consider each statement carefully. *Mark P for any statement you believe is provable. Mark U for any statement you feel is unprovable because of the lack of evidence. Mark C for statements you think are too controversial to be proved to everyone's satisfaction.*

If you are doing this activity as a member of a class or group, compare your answers with those of other class or group members. Be able to defend your answers. You may discover that others will come to different conclusions than you. Listening to the reasons others present for their answers may give you valuable insights in recognizing statements that are provable.

If you are reading this book alone, ask others if they agree with your answers. You too will find this interaction very valuable.

P = provable
U = unprovable
C = too controversial

1. Abortion is not a moral dilemma.
2. Many people find abortion repugnant.
3. Women who have abortions are primarily young and ignorant.
4. Biology will never have an answer to the question of when a fetus becomes a person.
5. A fetus becomes a person at birth.
6. No matter how charming a newborn baby is, no one is likely to come forth and offer to finance its Pampers or pay its college tuition.
7. No woman can forget a pregnancy no matter how it ends.
8. Many people cannot wholeheartedly support either the pro-choice or the anti-abortion groups.
9. The pro-life groups have a fear and an abhorrence of sex.
10. If teenagers did not engage in premarital sex, the teen pregnancy rate would be lowered.
11. Abortion is the taking of a human life.
12. There are a number of legal and socially acceptable ways to take human life.
13. No woman plans to have an abortion.
14. Men never experience pregnancy.
15. Religious persons have diverse views on abortion.
16. Not to take a stand on abortion is to already take a stand.
17. Abortion is always tragic.
18. The Bible forbids abortion.
19. Making abortion illegal will not stop abortion.
20. Many unwanted pregnancies could have been avoided.

Periodical Bibliography

The following list of periodical articles deals with the subject matter of this chapter.

Kenneth Cauthen	"The Legitimacy and Limits of Freedom of Choice," *The Christian Century*, July 1/8, 1981.
Nelson Dawson	"Abortion and the Moral? " *New Guard*, Winter 1980/81.
Joseph F. Donceel	"Catholic Politicians and Abortion," *America*, February 2, 1985.
John Garvey	"Who Confers Value? The Continuing Abortion Debate," *Commonweal*, August 9, 1985.
Thomas C. Fox	"Abortion Issue Is Not So Simple," *National Catholic Report*, October 19, 1984.
Jonathan Glover	"Matters of Life and Death," *New York Review of Books*, May 30, 1985.
Donald Granberg	"What Does It Mean to Be 'Pro-Life'? " *The Christian Century*, May 12, 1982.
Jeffrey Hart	"Abortion Is Not a 'Religious Issue, ''' *Human Events*, October 13, 1984.
Nat Hentoff	"Private Conscience and Public Policy," *Village Voice*, September 11, 1984.
Madonna Kolbenschlag	"Abortion and Moral Consensus: Beyond Solomon's Choice," *The Christian Century*, February 20, 1985.
People Weekly	"As the Abortion Issue Reaches a Political Flashpoint, Two Catholic Experts Clash in Debate," October 22, 1984.
Rosemary Radford Ruether	"Catholics and Abortion: Authority vs. Dissent," *The Christian Century*, October 3, 1985.
Richard Taylor and Jeanne Caputo	"Abortion and Morality," *Free Inquiry*, Fall 1982.
Ernest van den Haag	"Humanity: The Central Question," *National Review*, September 6, 1985.

Can Abortion Be Justified?

1 VIEWPOINT

"For us, the diagnosis of Down syndrome was reason to choose abortion."

Congenital Disease Justifies Abortion

Rayna Rapp

Even when a pregnancy is a welcomed, planned event, the issue of abortion can still loom large. With many women postponing childbirth until their thirties and even forties, the probability of birth defects and congenital diseases rises. Because of this, many women elect to have amniocentesis, a test in which a sampling of amniotic fluid is withdrawn from the womb and a series of tests are done to determine abnormalities. If the test results are positive and the woman is carrying an abnormal fetus, she may choose to have an abortion. In the following viewpoint, Rayna Rapp was faced with just such an agonizing decision, and chose to abort. She ends with the plea that society develop an outlet for these women to be able to discuss their choice together.

As you read, consider the following questions:

1. While the author explains that she admires women who decide to have a baby, even though it is handicapped, she did not do it. Why not?
2. How was the author's experience different from her husband's?
3. If you were faced with this decision, what would you do? Why?

Rayna Rapp, "XYLO: A true story," in *Test-Tube Women: What Future for Motherhood*, edited by Rita Arditta et al. London: Routledge & Kegan Paul PLC, 1984. Reprinted with permission.

Mike called the fetus XYLO, XY for its unknown sex, LO for the love we were pouring into it. Day by day we fantasized about who this growing cluster of cells might become. Day by day, we followed the growth process in the myriad books that surround modern pregnancy for the over-35 baby boomlet. Both busy with engrossing work and political commitments, we welcomed this potential child with excitement, fantasy, and the rationality of scientific knowledge. As a Women's Movement activist, I had decided opinions about treating pregnancy as a normal, not a diseased condition, and we were fortunate to find a health care team—obstetrician, midwives, genetic counselor—who shared that view.

The early months of the pregnancy passed in a blur of exhaustion and nausea. Preoccupied with my own feelings, I lived in a perpetual underwater, slow motion version of my prior life. As one friend put it, I was already operating on fetal time, tied to an unfamiliar regimen of enforced naps, loss of energy, and rigid eating. Knowing the research on nutrition, on hormones, and on miscarriage rates among older pregnant women, I did whatever I could to stay comfortable.

I was 36 when XYLO was conceived, and like many of my peers, I chose to have amniocentesis, a prenatal test for birth defects such as Down syndrome, Tay-sachs disease, and sickle-cell anemia. . . . Both Mike and I knew about prenatal diagnosis from our friends' experiences, and from reading about it. Each year, more than 20,000 American women choose amniocentesis to detect birth defects. The procedure is performed betwen the sixteenth and twentieth weeks of pregnancy. . . . Most obstetricians, mine included, send their pregnant patients directly to the genetic division of a hospital where counseling is provided, and the laboratory technicians are specially trained. Analysis of amniotic fluid requires complex laboratory work, and can cost between $400 and $1,000.

Fear of Down Syndrome

It was fear of Down syndrome that sent us to seek prenatal diagnosis of XYLO. Down syndrome produces a characteristic physical appearance—short, stocky size, large tongues, puffy upward slanting eyes with skin folds in the inner corners and is a major cause of mental retardation, worldwide. People with Down syndrome are quite likely to have weak cardiovascular systems, respiratory problems, and run a greater risk of developing childhood leukemia. While the majority of Down syndrome infants used to die very young, a combination of antibiotics and infant surgery enables modern medicine to keep them alive. And programs of childhood physical-mental stimulation may facilitate their assimilation. Some parents also opt for cosmetic surgery—

an expensive and potentially risky procedure. Down syndrome is caused by an extra chromosome, at the twenty-first pair of chromosomes, as geneticists label them. And while the diagnosis of Down spells mental retardation and physical vulnerability, no geneticist can tell you how seriously affected your particular fetus will be. There is no cure for Down syndrome. A pregnant woman whose fetus is diagnosed as having the extra chromosome can either prepare to raise a mentally retarded and physically vulnerable child, or decide to abort it. . . .

Abortion's Legal Limits

The waiting period for amniocentesis results is a long one, and I was very anxious. Cells must be cultured, then analyzed, a process that takes two or four weeks. We wait, caught between the late date at which amniocentesis can be performed (16 to 20 weeks); the moment of quickening, when the woman feels the fetus move (roughly 18 to 20 weeks), and the legal limits of abortion (very few of which are performed after 24 weeks in the United States). Those of my friends who have had amniocentesis report terrible fantasies, dreams, and crying fits, and I was no exception: I dreamed in lurid detail of my return to the lab, of awful damage. I woke up frantic, sobbing, to face the nagging fear that is focused in the waiting period after amniocentesis.

Confronting the Decision to Abort

How could I bring this person, whose life expectancy was 60 years, into the world, watching him suffer and not understand? But how could I abort and live with my guilt? . . .

Unless the child was institutionalized, I would have to give up my teaching to be a full-time nurse, putting the entire financial burden on [my husband] Bud. We would have to begin saving immediately for that day, in our old age, when we could no longer care for the child at home. While we might have somehow coped had we never had the tests, Bud couldn't fathom knowingly bringing these burdens upon us. . . . I decided I must go through with the abortion to preserve my family.

Maria Vida Hunt, *McCall's*, July 1985.

For the 98 percent of women whose amniotic fluid reveals no anomaly, reassurance arrives by phone, or more likely, by mail, confirming a negative test. When Nancy called me 12 days after the tap, I began to scream as soon as I recognized her voice; in her office, I knew only positive results (very negative results, from a potential parent's point of view) are reported by phone. The image of myself, alone, screaming into a white plastic telephone is indelible. Although it only took 20 minutes to locate Mike and bring him and a close friend to my side, time is suspended in my memory. I replay the call, and my screams echo for indefinite periods. We learned, after contacting our midwives and obstetrician, that a tentative diagnosis of a male fetus with Down syndrome had been made. Our fantasies for XYLO, our five months' fetus, were completely shattered.

Mike and I had discussed what we would do if amniocentesis revealed a serious genetic condition long before the test. For us, the diagnosis of Down syndrome was reason to choose abortion. Our thinking was clear, if abstract, long before the question became reality. We were eager to have a child, and prepared to change our lives to make emotional, social, and economic resources available. But the realities of raising a child who could never grow to independence would call forth more than we could muster, unless one or both of us gave up our work, our political commitments, our social existence beyond the household. And despite a shared commitment to coparenting, we both understood that in this society, that one was likely to be the mother. When I thought about myself, I knew that in such a situation, I would transform myself to become the kind of 24-hour-a-day advocate such a child would require. I'd do the best and most loving job I could, and I'd undoubtedly become an activist in support of the needs of disabled children.

No Support for the Disabled

But other stark realities confronted us: to keep a Down syndrome child alive through potentially lethal health problems is an act of love with weighty consequences. As we ourselves age, to whom would we leave the person XYLO would become? Neither Mike nor I have any living kin who are likely to be young enough, or close enough, to take on this burden after our deaths. In a society where the state provides virtually no decent, humane services for the mentally retarded, how could we take responsibility for the future of our dependent Down syndrome child? In good conscience, we couldn't choose to raise a child who would become a ward of the state. The health care, schools, various therapies that Down syndrome children require are inadequately available, and horrendously expensive in America; no single family should have to shoulder all the burdens that a decent health and social policy may someday extend to physically and mentally disabled people. In the meantime, while struggling for such a society, we did not choose to bring a child into this world who could never grow up to care for himself.

Most women who've opted for amniocentesis are prepared to face the question of abortion, and many of us *do* choose it, after a diagnosis of serious disability is made. Perhaps 95 percent of Down syndrome pregnancies are terminated after test results are known. Reports on other diseases and conditions are harder to find, but in one study, the diagnosis of spina bifida led to abortion about 90 percent of the time.

In shock and grief, I learned from my obstetrician that two kinds of late second-trimester abortions were available. Most common are the "installation procedures"—saline solution or urea is injected into the uterus to kill the fetus, and drugs are sometimes used to bring on labor. The woman then goes through labor to deliver the fetus. The second kind of mid-trimester abortion, and the one I chose, is a D&E—dilation and evacuation. This procedure demands more active intervention from a doctor, who vacuums out the amniotic fluid, and then removes the fetus. The D&E requires some intense, upsetting work for the medical team, but it's over in about 20 minutes, without putting the woman through labor. Both forms of late abortion entail some physical risk, and

---

A Nightmare Begins

A person's life can be turned into a nightmare with just a few words. My obstetrician was on the line, informing me that the results of the amniocentesis indicated the baby was severely abnormal, with forty-seven chromosomes instead of the normal forty-six. . . .

I managed to live through the day until [my husband] Jim came home. After much discussion and soul-searching, we decided that termination of the pregnancy was the only course. Every person deserves a fair chance at a good life, and this child wouldn't have that chance. He would also be an outcast, the object of stares and pity, perhaps even ridicule. He would never be a playmate for Jennifer [our daughter]; instead he'd be a lifelong burden, a burden we had no right to place on her. We had a responsibility to provide Jennifer with as normal and happy a childhood as possible, and we would be failing in that responsibility if we brought this child into the world. We knew that we couldn't cope with the havoc and devastation that visits families with children who are severely deformed and retarded.

Julie K. Ivey, *Glamour,* May 1982.

---

the psychological pain is enormous. Deciding to end the life of a fetus you've wanted and carried for most of five months is no easy matter. The number of relatively late second-trimester abortions performed for genetic reasons is very small, perhaps up to 400 a year. It seems an almost inconsequential number, unless you happen to be one of them.

Making the medical arrangements, going back for counseling, the pretests, and finally, the abortion, was the most difficult period of my adult life. I was then 21 weeks pregnant, and had been proudly carrying my expanding belly. Telling everyone—friends, family, students, colleagues, neighbors—seemed an endless nightmare. But it also allowed us to rely on their love and support during this terrible time. Friends streamed in from all over to teach my classes; I have scores of letters expressing concern; the phone never stopped ringing for weeks. Our community was invaluable, reminding us that our lives were rich and filled with live despite this loss. A few weeks afterward, I spoke with another woman who'd gone through selective abortion (as this experience is antiseptically called in medical jargon). She'd returned to work immediately, her terrible abortion experience unspoken. Colleagues assumed she'd had a late miscarriage, and didn't speak about it. Her isolation only underlined my appreciation of the support I'd received.

A Need for Handicapped Support Services

My parents flew a thousand miles to sit guard over my hospital bed, answer telephones, shop, and cook. Filled with sorrow for the loss of their first grandchild, my mother told me of a conversation she'd had with my father. Despite their grief, they were deeply grateful for the test. After all, she reasoned, we were too young and active to be devastated like this; if the child had been born, she and my dad would have taken him to raise in their older years, so we could get on with raising other children. I can only respond with deep love and gratitude for the wellspring of compassion behind that conversation. But surely, no single woman, mother or grandmother, no single family, nuclear or extended, should have to bear all the burdens that raising a seriously disabled child entails. It points out, once again, the importance of providing decent, humane attention and services for other-than-fully-abled children and adults.

And, of course, parents of disabled children are quick to point out that the lives they've nurtured have been worth living. I honor their hard work and commitments, as well as their love, and I think that part of "informed consent" to amniocentesis and selective abortion should include information about parents' groups of Down syndrome children, and social services available to them, not just the individual, medical diagnosis of the problem. And even people who feel they could never choose a late abortion may nonetheless want amniocentesis so they'll have a few extra months to prepare themselves, other family members, friends, and special resources for the birth of a child with special, complex needs.

Recovering from the abortion took a long time. Friends, family, coworkers, students did everything they could to ease me through the experience. Even so, I yearned to talk with someone who'd "been there." Over the next few months, I used my personal and medical networks to locate and talk with a handful of other women who'd opted for selective abortions. In each case, I was the first person they'd ever met with a similar experience. The isolation of this decision and its consequences is intense. Only when women (and concerned men) speak of the experience of selective abortion as a tragic but chosen fetal death can we as a community offer the support, sort out the ethics, and give the compassionate attention that such a loss entails.

For two weeks, Mike and I breathed as one person. His distress, loss, and concern were never one whit less than my own. But we were sometimes upset and angered by the unconscious attitudes toward his loss. He was expected to "cope," while I was nurtured through my "need." We've struggled for male responsibility in birth control, sexual mutuality, childbirth and child-rearing, and I think we need to acknowledge that those men who do engage in such transformed practice have mourning rights during a pregnancy loss, as well.

Nonetheless, our experiences *were* different, and I'm compelled to recognize the material reality of my experience. Because it happened in my body, a woman's body, I recovered much more slowly than Mike did. By whatever mysterious process, he was able to damp back the pain, and throw himself back into work after several weeks. For me, it took months. As long as I had the 14 pounds of pregnancy weight to lose, as long as my aching breasts, filled with milk, couldn't squeeze into bras, as long as my tummy muscles protruded, I was confronted with the physical reality of being post-pregnant, without a child. Mike's support seemed inadequate; I was still in deep mourning while he seemed distant and cured. Only much later, when I began doing research on amniocentesis, did I find one study of the stresses and strains of selective abortion. In a small sample of couples, a high percentage separated or divorced following this experience. Of course, the same holds true after couples face a child's disablement, or child death. Still, I had no idea that deep mourning for a fetus could be so disorienting. Abortion after prenatal diagnosis has been kept a medical and private experience, so there is no common fund of knowledge or support to alert us as individuals, as couples, as families, as friends, to the aftermath our "freedom of choice" entails.

Lift the Veil of Privacy

Which is why I've pierced my private pain to raise the issue. As feminists, we need to speak from our seemingly private experience toward a social and political agenda. I'm suggesting we lift the veil of privacy and professionalism to explore issues of health care, abortion, and the right to choose death, as well as life, for our genetically disabled fetuses. If XYLO's story, a true story, has helped to make this a compelling issue for more than one couple, then his five short months of fetal life will have been a great gift.

2 VIEWPOINT

"Some think that death might be the best option for some handicapped children because they think real people are 'normal' people."

Congenital Disease Does Not Justify Abortion

Melinda Delahoyde

Melinda Delahoyde is the former director of education of Americans United for Life and was co-editor of *Infanticide and the Handicapped Newborn*, an authoritative collection of essays on the issue of infanticide. A mother of a Down's Syndrome child, Ms. Delahoyde devotes herself to fighting against infant euthanasia and abortion. In the following viewpoint, Ms. Delahoyde explains her belief that in modern society, everything is geared toward perfection. Often the decision to abort an imperfect child is rooted in society's attitude that any person less than perfect is a cumbersome burden that is less than fully human. She believes that society must accept and love handicapped children, for it is only when we love the handicapped that we can truly value every human life.

As you read, consider the following questions:

1. How do many in our society view children, according to the author?
2. What anecdote does the author relate to show that normal is a relative term? How does this apply to the issue of abortion?

Most of us never enter the world of the handicapped persons. Ninety-six percent of children in this country are born "normal." Handicapped people are "different." We all have a natural aversion to someone we don't understand, to someone who does not or cannot act in the same way we act.

Some think that death might be the best option for some handicapped children because they think real people are "normal" people. They also think that being different means being less. Both of these attitudes are common in our society and both of them are worth examining to help us understand this issue.

Accustomed to Perfection

We are a nation accustomed to perfection. Our application of technology coupled with ever-growing affluence has given us "the best of everything." Everything should always work. When it doesn't work we throw it away. When we want something, we expect to get it now.

The expectation of having everything we want and having it work perfectly spills over into our attitudes toward children. Children are no longer viewed as an indispensable and totally natural part of life. We no longer ask a young couple "When are you going to have children?" but "*Are* you going to have children?" For many people, having children has to be balanced against the new condominium in the mountains or the second car they won't be able to have if they have a baby. Children for many have become ornaments that they choose to add to their lives.

I have seen this attitude in several close friends. These talented young women are rising to top spots in their careers. Unmarried, they have always had time to devote to travel and the long hours necessary to be successful in their professions. Yet now, in their early thirties they find themselves with a strong desire to have a baby. These women talk often about the experience of having a baby. It's clear that the feeling of giving birth and being a mother is more important than a husband, family, or even the actual baby. In other words, parenthood for them is a very self-centered experience. They want to have a child before it's too late because they don't want to miss out on something. They have had the best of everything until now and a child will complete their dream of the perfect life.

Expecting Normality

Naturally, these women expect their child to be "normal." In a plan so carefully prepared and calculated, a handicapped child is not welcome. These women are achievement-oriented professionals and they would expect the same from their children. If the child isn't normal then abortion, or even infanticide, could become the chosen "treatment option."

Of course not every young professional couple or single career woman has imbibed these attitudes of liberal motherhood. Happily, the bonds of parental love and maternal affection are often stronger than these ideas. Mothers can sacrifice for their children in spite of what they have been taught. But the idea of perfection runs deep in the present generation and it contributes to a cultural climate that condones infanticide.

Several years ago I met a young couple at a gathering of lawyers. Both were attorneys and the woman was five months pregnant. As we talked she told me that she had recently had an amniocentesis test and was waiting to see if her child was "normal." I asked her what she would do if the test revealed her baby had a handicap. Her quick answer was abortion. In fact she had had an abortion the previous year because their careers had made having a child inconvenient.

Reprinted by permission: Tribune Media Services.

This woman told me that she and her husband just did not have room in their lives for a handicapped child. What would have happened if their test had failed and the baby was born with a handicap? No one can say what they would have chosen. But we do know that the odds were stacked against the child from the beginning. Choosing life in this case would have been difficult at best.

We want what we want when we want it and we want it to be perfect. In that world view a child with a handicap just doesn't have a chance.

Why is it that perfection is often our only standard? Many times it is because we believe that being different means being less. A "normal" child and a "normal" adult do certain things. Those who cannot do these things are less of a human being.

I read about a couple who had decided to keep their baby boy with Down's Syndrome. They considered an abortion when they learned several months before birth that their child carried the Down's trait. But they had decided that their love and home was the best place for their child.

In the course of their decision-making they consulted with the director of a home for handicapped citizens. The parents kept telling the director about the things their child would never be able to do. He would never go to the prom, or play high school football, or go to college. To every comment like this the director's answer was the same: "But many normal children never do that." Finally the child's mother understood. "But what is normal?" she asked.

That is exactly the point. "Normal" is a very relative and subjective term. Indeed, it can be a meaningless term. Every person varies according to potential and capabilities. Just because a person cannot do some task does not mean he is less of a human being. Capabilities vary from person to person but humanity is there in full from the beginning. We often judge individuals in terms of their abilities and then set a standard for what every "normal" person should be. Instead, we should be looking at each person as a unique human being with a unique potential to fulfill. Our task is to help that person fulfill their potential, whatever it might be.

A friend told me about a visit he had with a family in Indiana. My friend has been active in the pro-life movement and had gone to Indiana to fulfill a speaking engagement. A woman had invited him to her home because she thought a visit with their two year old daughter might encourage my friend in his work.

A Hopeless Case

At the home of this farm family he found a beautiful two-year-old girl dressed in a blue sailor suit sleeping in her crib. But this child was really quite different. She was born with major portions of her brain missing. In fact, if you held her head close to a light you could almost see through to the back of her head. Doctors diagnosed her as a "hopeless case," but this farm family had adopted the baby girl and showered their love and faith upon her.

The girl had made great progress. At two years of age she was able to communicate her needs through different sounds, listen responsively to different kinds of music and gaze intently into her mother's eyes, even though she has no optic nerve. Doctors are convinced that she does, in some sense, see. They had predicted she would never be able to move and yet now she can lift up her head. The strides this child has made are nothing short of miraculous. Much of the credit must go to the love of her parents.

But as this mother talked with my friend it was obvious that her child's accomplishments were secondary to her. She had brought my friend to see the full humanity of this little girl. By most standards her accomplishments were minimal. She would never be a "normal child." But as her mother commented, "Her soul is completely whole." When this woman looked at her child she saw a complete human being. Although her physical and mental capacities were limited, her character, her essential personhood were fully present.

A Perfect Child: Not Constitutionally Guaranteed

Lots of women—and they keep increasing in number—have abortions for reasons that have nothing whatever to do with how much money they have. . . .

Especially now that more women under 35 are undergoing amniocentesis, the choice is abortion because the kid down there is going to be retarded. Or the kid has some other defect. And since everyone wants a perfect baby—it's guaranteed in the Constitution, isn't it?—the kid is done away with.

Nat Hentoff, *The Village Voice*, October 2, 1984.

Many times we practice a subtle yet powerful form of discrimination against our handicapped citizens by believing that being different means being less. I saw this kind of attitude illustrated in a discussion with college students about a hypothetical "life boat" situation they had been discussing in an ethics class. Twelve people were on a life boat and only seven could be saved. It was important to pick the right seven because a nuclear holocaust had destroyed the world and the seven survivors would have to create a new civilization. The candidates included among others, a priest, a social worker, a mathematician and a handicapped person.

Sacrificing the Handicapped

For many the handicapped person was the first to be sacrificed. After all, only the strongest, the fittest, the "best" were needed in the new world. The handicapped survivor would be a burden. In their eyes he was "of less value" than the other survivors. But several students chose the handicapped man first to remain in the life boat. It was difficult for them to put their reasons into words, but they were convinced that this person had something important and uniquely his own to contribute to the new society. In their opinion being different did not mean being less.

Often we think we have so much to offer our handicapped

citizens. But many times it is they who have so much to offer us. They can show us the courage, determination and perseverance that they have developed from painstakingly learning so many tasks we take for granted. Hasn't each of us seen moral courage illustrated by a blind man "seeing" his way along a sidewalk with a white cane? Handicapped people demonstrate to us the simplicity, joy, and love of a life that has been stripped of the striving for status and prestige that consumes so many of us.

Contributing to Society

A pastor friend of ours lost his oldest daughter to a brain tumor. A week after her death he returned to his congregation to preach the Sunday morning service. After the service many parishioners found it difficult to talk to their pastor. But one young handicapped man did understand that the pastor had lost someone he loved very much. This young man, who has very limited language skills, came up, put his arm around the pastor, and pointed to his own shoulder. He was letting the pastor know that he cared and if he wanted to put his head on his shoulder and have a good cry, it was fine with him. That young man, in his simple and loving way, expressed the thoughts of so many in that congregation that day. . . .

But if we uphold our ideas of the dignity and worth of every human life and publicly state our views, we can stop. . .injustice. Perhaps we all need to rethink our ideas about what it means to be a person and make a contribution in society.

VIEWPOINT 3

"If abortion can reduce the number of illegitimate and unwanted children it can reduce the potential for future homicides and child abuse."

The Unwanted Child Is Justification for Abortion

James W. Prescott

Many argue that while society can force women to bear children, it can never force them to love those children. If abortion is made a more difficult choice, society would condemn countless children to be born into a life of chronic abuse and neglect. In the following viewpoint, James W. Prescott argues that abortion reduces the frequency of child abuse by allowing those women to abort who would otherwise abuse their unwanted infants. Written ten years ago, it remains an eloquent plea for protecting the right to abortion. Mr. Prescott is a developmental neuropsychologist with the National Institute of Child Health and Human Development of Health and Human Services (HHS), Washington, DC, and served as a member of the Maryland House of Delegates Judiciary Committee's Subcommittee on Abortion Reform from 1967-1968.

As you read, consider the following questions:

1. What types of social problems will an unwanted child face, according to the author?
2. Why does the author argue that an unwanted child would be better off if he or she had never been born?
3. How are the studies Mr. Prescott cites relevant to his abortion stance?

James W. Prescott, "Abortion or the Unwanted Child: A Choice for a Humanistic Society." This article first appeared in THE HUMANIST issue of March/April 1975 and is reprinted by permission.

The anti-abortion movement believes that the fetus, even in its embryonic stage of development, is human life and that any deliberate termination of embryonic or fetal life constitutes an "unjustified" termination of human life—that is, homicide. Conversely, proponents of abortion deny that the fetus is human life, particularly during its embryonic stage of development, and therefore believe that the termination of fetal life does not constitute homicide. Further, proponents of abortion justify the termination of fetal life by asserting that the woman has the ultimate right to control her own body; that no individual or group of individuals has any right to force a woman to carry a pregnancy that she does not want; that parents have the moral responsibility and constitutional obligation to bring into this world only children who are wanted, loved, and provided for, so that they can realize their human potential; and that children have certain basic human and constitutional rights, which include the right to have loving, caring parents, sound health, protection from harm, and a social and physical environment that permits healthy human development and the assurance of "life, liberty, and the pursuit of happiness."

These conflicts of "rights"—namely, the presumed rights of the fetus, the rights of the woman, the rights of the child, the presumed rights of adults to unlimited reproduction, and the rights of society—need careful consideration in evaluating the morality of abortion. How do we order the priorities of competing "rights"? Since rights confer obligations, does the failure to meet those obligations mitigate or abrogate the rights that gave rise to those obligations?

Children's Rights and Abortion

For example, when conception occurs in a uterine environment known to be adverse or a child is permitted to be born into an adverse environment, both of which threaten or deny the child's basic human and constitutional rights and opportunities for normal human development, should moral and constitutional questions be raised concerning the rights of such parentage? Is the right to parentage absolute? Do adults who are incapable of responsible behavior (for example, the severely mentally retarded) have the right to bring into this world children who will be neglected and abused and who will become infant-and child-mortality statistics? Is it not more moral and humane to prevent a life than to permit a life that may experience deprivation, suffering, and perhaps a brutal early death, which many of our child-abuse and infant-and child-mortality statistics reflect? Is mere physical existence our highest goal and greatest moral burden? Or is the quality of human life our highest goal and greatest moral burden? What are the social and moral criteria for justifying the sacrifice of human life? Perhaps the justifications for a "just war" should be considered in relation to certain arguments for and against abortion.

These questions of moral behavior, like that of abortion itself, are unlikely to be resolved by religious convictions or theological doctrine, since such convictions and doctrine vary considerably among free people and are, at best, arbitrary in their formulation and implementation. The extensive debates on abortion clearly indicate that no philosophical, religious, or scientific consensus exists concerning the question of whether fetal life is human life. A similar lack of consensus exists concerning the moral and ethical nature of the abortive act. . . .

Life Worse Than Death

Legal or not, women will continue to have abortions because, as pro-woman advocates point out, there is no way legislation can make a woman or a man want an unwanted child. A life is not fully a life until it has been loved. What women know is that bringing an unwanted child into the world is the beginning of death not life. Legislation, then, that will compel them to give birth to unwanted children is not pro-life, but pro-death.

Joy M.K. Bussert, Minnesota Council of Churches, 1982.

Consequently, it would appear constructive to examine the abortion question from a different perspective. Specifically, what are the effects of denied abortions—that is, of compulsory childbirth or of being an unwanted child—upon the development of the child; what are the consequences to society when parents are denied the right to have only wanted children; and what are the characteristics of societies that permit abortion in contrast to those that punish abortion. An examination of these questions from the perspective of the behavioral and social sciences, rather than from that of theology, should provide a basis to evaluate the merits of abortion on different grounds and to clarify the motivations and some of the social and psychological characteristics of the pro-abortion and anti-abortion personality.

Consequences of Denied Abortion

One of the most important studies that tried to evaluate the consequences of being an unwanted child upon the development of the child was conducted in 1966 by H. Forssman and I. Thuwe of the Department of Psychiatry at Goteburg University in Sweden. Therapeutic abortion was offically legalized in Sweden in 1939 and liberalized in 1946 to include mental-health criteria. These Swedish investigators examined the development of children from birth to age twenty-one who were born during the years 1939 to 1941 to mothers who had applied for abortion but were denied. The sample included one hundred and twenty children, who were compared with a control group of children whose mothers had not applied for abortion. Of the unwanted children, 27 percent were born out of wedlock, whereas only 8 percent of the control children were born out of wedlock.

The statistically significant differences between the unwanted and the control children can be summarized as follows:

1. Sixty percent of the unwanted children had an insecure childhood, in contrast to only 28 percent of the control children. Criteria for an insecure childhood included official reports about unsatisfactory home conditions: the child was removed from the home by authorities; the child was placed in a foster or children's home; the parents were divorced or deceased before the child was fifteen; the child was born out of wedlock and never legitimized.
2. Twenty-eight percent of the unwanted children had received some form of psychiatric care, compared to 15 percent of the control children.
3. Eighteen percent of the unwanted children were registered with child-welfare boards for delinquency, compared to 8 percent of the control children.
4. Fourteen percent of the unwanted children had some form of higher education, compared to 33 percent of the control children.
5. Fourteen percent of the unwanted children received some form of welfare between the ages of sixteen and twenty-one, in contrast to 2.5 percent of the control children.
6. And finally, while 68 percent of the control children showed none of the social disabilities mentioned above, only 48 percent of the unwanted children were free of such characteristics.

It is worth noting that many of the differences listed were found in different social classes. In summary, unwanted children are more than twice as likely to suffer the social, emotional, and educational disadvantages as wanted children, on a variety of measures. Unwanted children appear to present certain costs to society: increased delinquency, a higher number of welfare recipients, a more poorly educated citizenry, and a greater number of psychiatric problems.

Consequences of Being Unwanted

The killing of a child by its parents is an extreme outcome of being unwanted and is the final act of child abuse. Roman civil law recognized the right of the father to maim and kill his offspring (*patria potestas*), and a number of cultures have practiced the killing of female infants because they were valued less than male infants. Ceremonial sacrifices of infants and children have been documented in a number of cultures, and Abraham's willingness to kill his son for religious purposes is a biblical case in point. But the killing of one's own child in a modern civilization is uniformly met with revulsion and horror—even though child abuse, which is the precursor of filicide (the killing of one's own children) and neonaticide (the killing of the newborn), is widespread today. The central issue here is the role of abortion in preventing unwanted children and helping reduce the incidence of child abuse and infanticide. . . .

Phillip J. Resnick, in a study of one hundred thirty-one filicides, found that 49 pecent were associated with "altruistic" motives—for example, to relieve suffering; 21 percent were attributed to parental psychoses; 26 percent were attributed to the child's being "unwanted," which includes the child-abuse syndrome, and 4 percent were attributed to revenge on the spouse. Statistics, however, fail to convey the horror and tragedy of parents killing their own children, particularly when it could be prevented.

Several of the case histories are so grueling that they cannot help but raise the question of whether it is more humane to prevent human life than to compel it into an existence that possibly could result in a cruel and painful death. Dr. Resnick cites several means by which infants and children are killed. He states: "Head trauma, strangulation, and drowning were the most frequent methods of filicide. Fathers tended to use more active methods, such as striking, squeezing, or stabbing, whereas mothers more often drowned, suffocated, or gassed their victims."

A Prominent Abortion Myth

Most unwanted pregnancies become wanted children. Women make mistakes having abortions.

Many unwanted children are abused, neglected and/or battered by unloving or immature parents. Some are killed or abandoned after birth by women who delivered alone. Many women make mistakes in having babies they don't want and can't love or care for.

National Abortion Rights Action League, *Legal Abortion: Arguments Pro and Con.*

It is unnecessary to catalogue the atrocities that are sometimes inflicted upon unwanted children. In Dr. Resnick's study of thirty-seven neonaticides, he found that *83 percent of infant killings were attributed to being "unwanted" by the mother;* 11 percent to psychoses; 3 percent to "accidental" murder (child abuse); and 3 percent to "altruism." These infanticides must be seriously considered in any discussion of abortion, since for some people they may seem to be the only alternative to compulsory pregnancies. . . .

The common factors associated with infant mortality, illegitimacy, and homicide assume greater significance in the context of the findings of J. Sklar and B. Berkov, who demonstrated that legalized abortion reduces the number of illegitimate babies. They reported that for the year 1971 an estimated thirty-nine thousand more illegitimate babies and twenty-eight thousand more legitimate babies would have been born if legalized abortion had not been available. It was emphasized that the illegitimate births prevented represent almost one-tenth of all out-of-wedlock children born in the country in 1971. Two other effects of legalized abortion were reported: (1) a reduction of the incidence of pregnancy-related marriages and subsequent marital disruption; and (2) the prevention of illegal abortions, since it was estimated that between two-thirds and three-fourths of all legal abortions in the United States in 1971 were replacements for illegal abortions. These authors concluded that a return to restrictive and repressive abortion laws would result in an increase in illegal abortions, pregnancy-related marriages, and illegitimacy.

Since illegitimacy has been linked to adult homicide and the killing of unwanted infants, it is clear that if abortion can reduce the number of illegitimate and unwanted children it can reduce the potential for future homicides and child abuse.

A Humanitarian Act

Given the alternative to abortion—that is, the birth of unwanted children, with all the adverse implications—it is clear that abortion is a beneficent and humanitarian act that values the *quality* of future human life more than the *quantity* of future human life. It is worth mentioning that the principle of the prevention of human life has its precedent in scripture—albeit in a different context—namely, Judas' betrayal of Jesus Christ: "It had been good for that man if he had not been born" (Matthew 26:24). Should this not be equally true for many children who are doomed to a life of misery and abuse, and for some who may meet an early violent death? . . .

These data strongly support the right of the woman to be pregnant by choice and to be a mother by choice as essential prerequisites for a humane and compassionate society.

4 VIEWPOINT

"An unwanted pregnancy does not lead regularly to an unwanted child."

An Unwanted Child Is Not a Reason for Abortion

James Tunstead Burtchaell

James Tunstead Burtchaell is a noted scholar and teacher, with degrees from Cambridge University, the Pontificia Universita Gregoriana in Rome, and the University of Notre Dame. Provost at Notre Dame until his retirement in 1977, he is still an active member of the university's Department of Theology. He has served as the president of the American Academy of Religion and is the author or editor of numerous works, including two on abortion, *Abortion Parley*, and his most recent, from which this viewpoint is excerpted, *Rachel Weeping: And Other Essays on Abortion*. In the viewpoint, Father Burtchaell argues that the unwanted child is not necessarily an abused and neglected child after birth. Many women learn to love and are delighted with the children they did not plan.

As you read, consider the following questions:

1. What is wrong with many of the studies that claim an unwanted child is an abused and neglected child, according to the author?
2. Why does the author believe that legal abortion increases child abuse?
3. What reasons does the author give to support his belief that parents must make their needs secondary to that of their child's?

When one has stripped off the claims of medical and psychiatric need for abortion—claims that were generated with an eye to legal clearance and public approval—there remains the one innermost indication, or reason, for abortion as currently practiced: that children are sometimes not wanted. The prevailing motive for abortion, . . . is that the mother, on her own determination or through the intervention of persons persuasive with her, does not welcome the unborn she is carrying. The argument on her behalf is that no woman ought to be forced to give birth to a son or daughter whom she does not welcome.

This claim takes several shapes. Sometimes it is pled on the child's behalf. "Without legal and affordable abortion," editorializes *Time* magazine, "many lives in progress are hopelessly ruined; the unwanted children very often grow up unloved, battered, conscienceless, trapped and criminal. A whole new virus of misery breeds in the accidental zygotes." Without available abortion, "the women (often young girls) who cannot raise the money must presumably. . .bear their unwanted children—thus bringing many thousands of new customers to welfare." In this appeal, as in others, there is a clear implication that it is the poor who typically lack the wherewithal to raise their children decently and therefore also lack the willingness to bear more of them. Minnesota Abortion Rights Council president Betty Benjamin presses the point: "Among the 800,000 unplanned, unwanted children born every year in the U.S., many become loved and wanted. Unfortunately, many others end up as battered children, delinquents, and criminals. Studies of battered children reveal a high percentage of unmarried and unwanted pregnancy, or forced marriage among the abusive parents." Mrs. Benjamin does not refer us to these studies, but her impression is widely shared. It is contradicted by the research of E.F. Lenoski, pediatrician at the University of Southern California Medical School, who found that 90 percent of the battered or abused children he studied were the result of desired pregnancies, compared with only 63 percent of children in a matched control group. Also, battered children were much more likely to be born of legitimate birth, and to mothers who displayed satisfaction with their pregnancy. . . .

Studies of the "Unwanted"

In Sweden, Forssman and Thuwe traced 120 children whose mothers had sought unsuccessfully to abort them (study group) and compared them to 120 other children (control group). Study children at age twenty-one were found to have had a more insecure childhood (70 percent vs. 34 percent), more psychiatric care (28 percent vs. 15 percent), more reported delinquency (18 percent vs. 8 percent), more drunken misconduct (16 percent vs. 11 percent), less higher education (14 percent vs. 33 percent), more welfare payments in their later teens (14 percent vs. 3.5 percent), more rejections among males for military service (15 percent vs. 7 percent), and more subnormal grades in school (11 percent vs. 5 percent). James Prescott of the National Institutes of Health, testifying on behalf of abortion, concludes: "Unwanted children suffer over twice the social, emotional and mental disabilities than do wanted children on a variety of measures. The costs to society in increased crimes; welfare recipients; poorly educated citizenry and drunkenness constitute a clear and present danger to a well-functioning society." Dr. Leonard Laufe, an obstetrician and consultant to Planned Parenthood, draws a more vigorous conclusion: "There was an overwhelming significant portion of antisocial behavior among these children—the common criminal crimes that we all know, plus a very significant incidence of schizophrenia in those offspring."

The Sweden study has not enjoyed as much credit among social scientists as it has among abortion advocates. Forssman and Thuwe neglected to control, or isolate, the factor of illegitimacy. Many children in the "unwanted" study group were reared out of wedlock, a factor not matched in the control group, and one which by itself would heavily influence the children's welfare and development. The study, therefore, has been seen as inconclusive.

A Child's Value Is Intrinsic

This is not another discourse on the all-too-familiar arguments for and against abortion. It is, instead, an examination of what has come to be known as the "unwanted child" justification for abortion. . . .

We know from a number of quarters that there are as many persons waiting to adopt children as there are women aborting them, so why are such children deemed "unwanted"? My own children may be unwanted to others, but they are very much wanted by me. Were the situation reversed, would I then be justified in snuffing out their lives? Is the value of a child assigned or is it inalienable?

Cal Thomas, *The Washington Times*, April 19, 1985.

A second and more careful inquiry into the fortunes of unwanted children has been conducted in Czechoslovakia. The study children there number 220 and they were born to mothers who were denied abortion twice: their requests had been turned down, appealed, and again turned down. The control group, for comparison, was carefully assembled and matched. The unwanted children, over the years, have fallen behind the control children in a number of comparisons, leading Dr. Prescott to state that they "experienced quite varied and usually more unfavorable consequences in their subsequent lives than wanted children," and thus to argue "that denial of abortion leads to undesirable consequences for the unwanted child and society."

But here again the research is too exuberantly put to use. While advocates recount all comparisons disfavorable to the study group they fail to point out that on most comparisons the differences between the groups are too slight to be statistically significant, while on some scales the "unwanted" children rank higher, leading the researchers themselves to observe that the study children had not fared so badly. "The idea commonly held among psychiatrists and clinical psychologists that eventual difficulties in the behavior of an unwanted child are inevitably linked with the originally rejecting attitude of the mother toward his existence is not wholly supported for both boys and girls. On the other hand, the view commonly entertained by the lay public that the birth of the child changes everything and every mother comes to deeply love her child is apparently also invalid."

The Prague researchers began with the knowledge that "in child psychiatry and psychology the opinion is generally accepted that an unwanted pregnancy can have a very negative influence upon the development of a child." After straining to confirm this assumption, they admit that between these two meticulously studied groups of "unwanted" and "wanted" children, "the differences remain to be not very pronounced and not very dramatic." The most that they can conclude about unwantedness is that it "is a factor not nearly negligible in the life of the child.". . .

The most rigorous research into the ups and downs in the lives of children rejected during pregnancy does not show them to be blighted by adversity. They seem, on an honest reading of the studies, to be in arrears in some aspects of their lives, but far less than one might have anticipated, and decidedly less than would reasonably support the thought that society and the children would both be better off had the children been denied birth. Presumably even those willing to entertain the view that the unborn are being done a favor by extirpation would need evidence of a more dreadful destiny for them than these studies describe.

Mother's Acceptance

But even if the force of the "unwantedness" argument for abortion as an intervention on behalf of the child is stymied for want of evidence, it needs to be examined further. As many have pointed out, a woman who does not want the child she is carrying cannot be relied upon to continue in that attitude. . . . An unwanted pregnancy does not lead regularly to an unwanted child. . . .Evidence is surfacing that women (and men) who did not want to carry their unborn to term have later reported that they were satisfied as parents of those children. It is interesting to note what social scientists, especially those sympathetic towards abortion, do with this evidence. Some tend to disbelieve the reliabiltiy of the mothers' memories. Others disbelieve mothers who say they came to love their children, and conjecture that they must still be harboring unconscious hostility. . . .

[The] notion. . .that unintended conception yields an unwanted pregnancy and a repudiated child, has gained strong acceptance. It is the background of the creed of Planned Parenthood: "We believe that the birth of every child should never be an accident." It has led to casual estimates, well beyond theirs, of how many unwanted children see the light of day in America. And, as an arguing point on behalf of abortion, it has also influenced how many children do not see the light of day.

Abortion Associated with Child Abuse

An obvious question of method arises when a study systematically writes off the accumulated experience of parenthood as an increasing deviation from a younger, less accommodating wisdom. But it also invites some meditation on the widespread American belief that the finest possible preamble to a childhood that is happy, well provided for, and well adjusted is a pregnancy that is purposeful. A Canadian psychiatrist has speculated, for example, that it is abortion, not unwanted birth, which is associated with child abuse. Philip Ney, chief of psychiatry in a Vancouver hospital, noticed that an increase in child deaths from social causes in Canada coincided with the introduction of elective abortion; that provinces with high and low abortion rates rank similarly in child abuse; and that individual

Reprinted by permission of United Features Syndicate, Inc.

women who abused their children were reported to have higher abortion rates. "Having to treat so many battered children, I began to worry that using abortion to make every child a wanted child might be backfiring. When I examined the evidence, I became convinced that most of the abused children resulted from wanted pregnancies and that elective abortion is an important cause of child abuse." Ney offers several hypotheses to explain the relationship between elective abortion and the battered child syndrome:

> Having an abortion can interfere with a mother's ability to restrain her anger toward those depending on her care. Abortion might also weaken a social taboo against harming those who are defenseless. With wholesale abortions discarding nondefective unborn children, the value of children might diminish, resulting in less care and protection. . . .An aborting person, having already repressed her instinctive caring for her unborn young, might be less inhibited in giving vent to her rage at a whimpering child. . . .
>
> Only two decades ago parents were willing to suffer major deprivation to have and raise children. It seemed like a sacred obligation or a great privilege. Nowadays, people balance having children with wanting a country house, another car, better vacations and early retirement. This might be observed by children in such families. As a result they might feel less confidence in their parents' true concern for their welfare. They might then become so importunate in their demands for care and attention that their parents feel threatened. Not infrequently, the parental response to those attention-demanding children will be physical violence. . . .
>
> Society is beginning to believe that a child has no right to exist and is therefore valued only when it is wanted. If it is permissible to kill an unwanted, unborn child, then one can defend killing children already born when they are no longer considered valuable. . . .

Ney's suggestions enlarge a doubt that "wantedness" best describes what healthy parenthood requires. . . .

An Ideal Welcome?

The most profound question to be raised in this matter is this: is good parenthood—zestful, generous, expansive, resilient—most reliably vouched for by planned and purposeful pregnancy, if children inevitably require of their parents a continual acquiescence—a delight, even—in so much that is unplanned and unpurposeful? How ideal a welcome is it for a child to be born to parents at exactly the time and into exactly the life circumstances they have wished for him or her? Is it not a small step from there for them to decide further, when the choice is open to them, that they will welcome a him but not a her? . . .

Once one has got the fit and feel of it, one easily expects that she or he has a right to get the sort of child one dreams of: unblemished, right sex, high IQ—all that a parent could require. The snag in this is that the parental vocation knows no other phase or moment when children can or should conform absolutely to their parents' requirements. The mindset of untrammeled choice, of "wantingness," is at odds with true and hopeful parenthood, where there is much more coping than choosing to be done. . . .

A License to Kill

We are told that abortion is necessary for the sake of the unwanted, handicapped, or potentially abused child. This is, we must kill the child to save it! The child's "right to be born a wanted child" is subtly transformed into a license to kill it if unwanted.

Raymond J. Adamek, *USA Today*, May 1984.

With this sort of reaction in mind, columnist Sidney Callahan wrote in 1971:

> The powerful (including parents) cannot be allowed to want and unwant people at will. . . .
>
> It's destructive of family life for parents even to think in these categories of wanted and unwanted children. By using the words you set up parents with too much power, including psychological power, over their children. Somehow the child is being measured by the parent's attitudes and being defined by the parent's feelings. We usually want only objects, and wanting them or not implies that we are superior, or at least engaged in a one-way relationship, to them.
>
> In the same way, men have "wanted" women through the ages. Often a woman's position was precarious and rested on being wanted by some man. The unwanted woman could be cast off when she was no longer a desirable object. She did not have an intrinsic dignity beyond wanting.

Rejection of Motherhood

In marriage, in childbearing, in all tightly bonded human relationships, it is a brittle and feckless attitude which orders up all things according to one's wants, and expects to see the adventure through on the same terms. Abortion because a child is unwanted has no ground to stand on that is truly in the child's favor. The only referent for the rejection is oneself: one does not want this child to live, to impinge. Some psychiatric researchers have seen this as profoundly selfish. One study, for instance, observes: "Contrary to the popular belief that shame over pregnancy out of wedlock is the major motivation for abortion, we observed that. . .much more important was the woman's rejecting of motherhood with all of its attendant demands. Our impression is that these women tend to be narcissistic and regard the fetus as a competitor for the succorance and dependent care they themselves obviously require." Another study noticed that women who approached abortion as an issue related to concerns of justice involving a weighing of two lives were more likely to continue their pregnancies, while women who approached abortion as an issue related to the self-determination of the individual were more likely to terminate their pregnancies. Arranging one's children for one's wants is hardly the model to put forward for nurturing parenthood. Indeed, some research has suggested that parents of battered children think of them very possessively, as positively "wanted."...

Children and Parental Needs

C. Henry Kempe, who coined the term "the battered-child syndrome" and has done extensive research in the abuse of children, has observed: "Basic in the abuser's attitude toward infants is the conviction, largely unconscious, that children exist in order to satisfy parental needs." This is why doctors in this field have been pointing out that prospective battering parents *want* children, and in this they stand apart from aborting parents. If the two groups have anything in common, it is "the assumption that the rights, desires, and ideas of the adult take full precedence over those of the child, and that children are essentially the property of parents who have the right to deal with their offspring as they see fit, without interference."

While it is obviously desirable that children be wanted when conceived, "unwantedness" fails as a convincing argument for abortion. Many children who were not wanted orginally cause a change of heart in their parents. Children born in the face of hostile animus from their parents are not crippled by that original unwantedness. There are no clear signs that children first unwanted face abuse. Indeed, some forms of pathological child treatment involve a possessive "wantedness." Healthy, adaptive parenthood must be prepared from the start to make one's own wants second to one's children's needs—including the need to go on living.

VIEWPOINT 5

"The reasons women choose abortion have not changed. It is still an operation that a woman chooses if she believes that it will improve her life."

Economics Is a Justification for Abortion

Barbara R. Bergmann

Barbara R. Bergmann is a professor of economics at the University of Maryland. In the following viewpoint, Ms. Bergmann speaks of her mother's abortions and concludes that abortion is primarily an economic decision for women. Confronted with the choice of remaining poor and dependent, a woman should be able to opt for abortion.

As you read, consider the following questions:

1. What was the author's first reaction to her mother's abortions?
2. How does the author believe illegal abortion would change women's roles?
3. Does the author believe that illegal abortions stop women from having abortions?

Barbara R. Bergmann, "The Economics of Abortion," *Los Angeles Times*, October 21, 1984. Reprinted with the author's permission.

If you want to get a new perspective on the abortion controversy, you might have a friendly and respectful conversation with your own mother. Don't start by asking her opinion on the personhood of the fetus. Ask her instead whether she ever had an abortion. If she has had one, ask her why. Her answer is likely to have more to do with economics than you might imagine.

When I was 22 my mother volunteered to me the fact that she had been through three abortions. It was a shock to hear my own mother, whom I knew as a warm and loving person, confessing to have done away with what I immediately personified as three brothers and sisters. Three people very like me, my own flesh and blood, who would have been close and dear relatives, had been cut off from life. I was not bothered by the thought of the pain to them of losing their lives, which I considered to be nil. What hurt was the thought that I had been cut off from them, and would have to live my life without them.

Economic Reasons

My mother's reasons, as she explained them to me, were mostly economic and therefore mostly "selfish." She did not want to spend her time and energy bringing up more children than the one whom she already had. She wanted to spend that time and energy in different ways—working, making money, enjoying herself. The cost of more children also was on her mind. She thought that she had better uses for the money that she would have had to spend on the extra children.

My mother's abortions were performed half a century ago. Today's abortions are very different, virtually painless and posing minimal risk. However, the reasons women choose abortion have not changed. It is still an operation that a woman chooses if she believes that it will improve her life.

If it had been in the government's power to force my mother to give birth to those three children against her will, convention would have forced her to raise them, and her life would have been very different. The government would have forced my mother to endure three more pregnancies, three more deliveries, three more rounds of diapers, and years and years more of non-stop child care than she was willing to endure. The family would have had a third less income and twice as many mouths to feed. The government would have imposed on my mother a very long sentence at hard labor in the prison of poverty for having sexual relations with her husband.

Abortion Improved Her Life

There is no doubt in my mind that those abortions did improve my mother's life, and that the millions of abortions every year to married and unmarried women improve the lives of those people in their own eyes. Of course, anyone has the right to believe that my mother and all the other millions of women who have undergone abortions were morally wrong. But most of those women who choose abortion do not believe that they have done any real harm to anyone, including the babies cut off from life.

If abortion were to become impossible again in this country, the lives of the vast majority of American women would worsen dramatically. Many would be forced to spend decades living a life that they did not want. For all women sexual activity, even within marriage, would become rife with hateful risk. The entire revolution in sex roles is built on low, controlled fertility. Without abortion women could not be in the labor force in increasing numbers, independent in increasing numbers and having meaningful careers. It is low fertility that makes day care economically feasible for many families.

Michael Keefe for the *Denver Post*, reprinted with permission.

The leaders of the anti-abortion campaign emphasize the fetus' loss of life. However, some of the same people oppose the revolution in sex roles, the new freedom to express sexuality, and would make birth control illegal if they could. Many of them make no secret of their desire to see women return to obligatory domesticity and to a situation in which they're afraid to have sex outside marriage. They believe that a ban on abortion would further that agenda.

It is certainly possible that Congress. . .will give the Catholic bishops their victory and make abortion once again a crime. However, there is so much at stake for women that there is little chance they will give up abortions. If they have to get them illegally, they will. To obtain her abortions, my mother had to endure the fear of death not after two months of life as a small ball of cells but 30 years into a conscious life. Today's women may have to go back to the same horror, but they will do it if they have to.

VIEWPOINT

6

"Why is it that we assume women are incapable of dealing with the adversity of an unwanted pregnancy by any other means than that of destroying life?"

Economics Is Not a Justification for Abortion

Janet E. Smith

In the following viewpoint, Janet E. Smith argues that when abortion is suggested for pregnant women in financial straits, society is practicing discrimination against women. Women can overcome economic burdens to have a child, and that child, as long as it is loved, will be no worse off for having grown up in poverty. Ms. Smith is an Assistant Professor at the University of Notre Dame in Indiana.

As you read, consider the following questions:

1. What two assumptions about the need for abortion does the author reject?
2. The author sees a contradiction between women's liberation's goals and its position on abortion. What is this contradiction?

Janet E. Smith, "Abortion as a Feminist Concern," *The Human Life Review*, Summer 1978. Reprinted with the author's permission.

Editor's note: The following viewpoint is excerpted from a longer article in which the author makes several points regarding abortion. This portion is excerpted from the end of the article.

The. . .final woman about whom I am going to speak did meet the "usual" description given by pro-abortionists. She was in her sixth month of pregnancy with her second child. She was twenty-seven, mother of a four-year-old, divorced, abandoned by the father of the second child—and trying to finish her college education. As we spoke she told me that absolutely everyone who knew she was pregnant had advised her to have an abortion: her doctor, the nurse, her friends. They all told her that it was irresponsible for her to bring another child into this world. She was poor, unmarried, and still unemployed and untrained. Others had told her that it took a great deal of money to raise a child. Her answer was that no one handed her a check as she emerged from the womb.

This woman was resolute in her determination to have her child. She said that since she had borne one child there was no chance of her having an abortion—no one could convince her to kill what she knew was life. She said she knew it would be hard but why should the child pay with its life for her mistake? Here was a woman willing to assume her responsibilities but who was being told that she was irresponsible. How many women could withstand such pressure? More important, why did her friends respond in such a fashion? Why was it *assumed* that she should not have the child? Why, instead of asking how they might help her keep her child, did her friends urge her to commit an act she knew to be killing? The answer, it seems to me, is based on two primary assumptions: that happiness depends upon a certain present and potential financial status, and that a mere woman could not cope with such adversity, i.e., we no longer believe that old maxim "love will find a way." I reject both assumptions.

Are the Poor Unhappy?

To holders of the first assumption, I address the question: are the poor necessarily unhappy? Furthermore, should we *kill* the poor rather than help them? It is popular nowadays in the U.S. to point out how costly it would be for the taxpayers to support the babies of welfare women if we do not pay for their abortions. So life does indeed have a price tag. And is our society really so impoverished that we are not able to assist the poor—that we would prefer that they abort their offspring rather than strain our pocketbooks? What kind of people have we become? Do we value human life so little, and, more in keeping with my argument here, why do we underrate our women so?

As to the second assumption: Why is it that we assume women are incapable of dealing with the adversity of an unwanted pregnancy by any other means than that of destroying life? Is this a flattering view of women? Is this a true view of women? Are women so weak psychologically that they cannot deal with what I so often hear referred to as the "trauma" of an unwanted pregnancy? I argue that by allowing women to abort their unwanted pregnancies we are telling them that we have a very low opinion of them. Isn't a mark of a mature and responsible person the ability to face problems squarely? Does not the mature person have the ability and the desire to consider the well-being of all those who are involved in a situation which presents problems—not just herself?

Only a Few Months

In fact, I take the legalization of abortion to be an indication that as a society we expect less of our women than we do of our men. After all, society has traditionally in times of war asked men to risk their own lives. But we are unwilling to ask women to offer a few months of their lives in order to give life. Why is it that we expect men to be able to risk their lives for the well-being of us all, while we do not ask a woman to give a few months to protect a life she is responsible for creating?

Social Pressure

A [frequent] theme which runs through the testimony of women traumatized by their abortion experience is anger at the pressure placed on them to abort their babies. Lori Nerad's abortion appointment was made by an employee of the Michigan Welfare Department, who intimated that if she refused to have an abortion her welfare checks might be cut off. "I've heard more and more stories from poor women and black women who've been pressured into abortion by welfare authorities," says Mrs. Nerad.

Maggie Gallagher, *Policy Review*, Spring 1985.

In this day of unparalleled opportunities for women, when women pride themselves on their ability to fend for themselves, when many agencies are designed for helping women in distress—why do we assume that women who become pregnant when inconvenient for them are not resourceful enough to find a way to nourish the life they have conceived? Or is it not a lack of resourcefulness—but a lack of love? And, as I have been arguing, a lack of love not only for the unborn child in whose creation the woman has played a part—but also of love for oneself for what she is; that is, a lack of love for being a woman and for the power which belongs exclusively to women, that of bearing children.

A popular saying in the women's movement claims that "women hold up half the sky." I would like to take the sentiment further and suggest that *only* women can hold up one particular half of the sky and thus it is necessary that women remain women. We cannot deny one important fact; women are the bearers of life, and thus it follows that they are entrusted with the protection and care of life, which, we might say, is their half of the sky. One of my male friends is fond of saying that his pregnant wife considers him merely a donor. In a very real sense, the future of humanity is in the hands of women, or, more specifically, in their wombs. We ought not, as women, to be demanding a world in which we may destroy freely the life we are capable of creating. Rather we ought to demand and work toward the goal of a world where life is safe for all.

a critical thinking skill

Recognizing Stereotypes

A stereotype is an oversimplified or exaggerated description of people or things. Stereotyping can be favorable. However, most stereotyping tends to be highly uncomplimentary, and, at times, degrading.

Stereotyping grows out of our prejudices. When we stereotype someone, we are prejudging him or her. Consider the following example: Mrs. Jones believes that all women who become pregnant without planning to are irresponsible and negligent in their use of birth control. The possibility that a woman's birth control method may have failed, or that a woman might become pregnant after being raped never occurs to her. Why not? Simply because she has prejudged all women who have had abortions and will keep her stereotype consistent with her prejudice.

The following statements relate to the subject matter in this chapter. Consider each statement carefully. *Mark S for any statement that is an example of stereotyping. Mark N for any statement that is not an example of stereotyping. Mark U if you are undecided about any statement.*

If you are doing this activity as a member of a class or group, compare your answers with those of other class or group members. Be able to defend your answers. You may discover that others will come to different conclusions than you. Listening to the reasons others present for their answers may give you valuable insights in recognizing stereotypes.

If you are reading this book alone, ask others if they agree with your answers. You too will find this interaction very valuable.

S = stereotype
N = not a stereotype
U = undecided

1. A woman who gives birth to a handicapped child is doing the right thing.
2. Many teenagers become pregnant because they are not using a reliable contraceptive method.
3. Some women would not be able to cope with the stress of taking care of a handicapped child.
4. A woman's natural, maternal instinct will win out even if she bears a child she does not want before birth.
5. Children with Down's syndrome are better off not being born.
6. A woman's career can interfere with her plans to have a child.
7. Women who are forced to bear children they do not want will both physically and psychologically abuse the child.
8. A typical abortion is performed on a poor, uneducated woman.
9. When a child is wanted, it is guaranteed to have a happy, healthy childhood.
10. A woman cannot respect life and have an abortion.
11. A poor woman can raise a child just as well as a wealthy woman.
12. Women who have abortions because the fetus has a congenital disease are selfish.
13. A child raised in poverty does not necessarily turn out to be a bad person.
14. A teenager should not raise a child.
15. Doctors who perform abortions are greedy, uncaring, and unethical.
16. Anti-abortionists' attitudes are governed by their religious beliefs.
17. A religious person is always against abortion.
18. Women cannot cope with poverty and therefore need the option of abortion.
19. Women are the bearers of life.

Periodical Bibliography

The following list of periodical articles deals with the subject matter of this chapter.

Deborah Baldwin	"Abortion: The Liberals Have Abandoned the Poor," *The Progressive*, September 1980.
Jessma O. Blockwick	"Pro-Choice Position Safeguards Basic and Treasured Values," *Engage/Social Action*, March 1983.
Janet Chase	"Not Quite the Baby I Expected. . . , " *Good Housekeeping*, October 1984.
Robert F. Drinan	"Life: To Defend It Means To Feed the Hungry, . . ." *National Catholic Reporter*, September 7, 1984.
John George	"Abortion and Free Choice," *Free Inquiry*, Vol. 5, No. 4, Fall 1985.
Nat Hentoff	"Some Kids Who Escaped from the Death Doctors," *Village Voice*, April 24, 1984.
Mary Meehan	"In Things Touching Conscience," *The Human Life Review*, Winter 1984. Available from 150 E Thirty-fifth St., New York, NY 10016.
Seventeen	"I Had an Abortion," *Seventeen*, October 1984.
Seventeen	"I Kept My Baby," *Seventeen*, October 1984.
Amanda Spake	"The Propaganda War Over Abortion," *Ms.*, July 1985.
Corinne Shear Wood	"For Women, the Abortion Dilemma Is a Question of How, Not If," *Los Angeles Times*, April 3, 1985.
Christopher Wolfe	"Abortion and Catholic Politicians," *Catholicism in Crisis*, October 1984.

CHAPTER 5

Should Abortion Remain Legal?

VIEWPOINT 1

"The single most important effect of legalization has been the substitution of safe, legal procedures for abortions that formerly were obtained illegally."

Legal Abortion Improves Public Health

Frederick S. Jaffe, Barbara L. Lindheim and Philip R. Lee

Frederick S. Jaffe is former president of The Alan Guttmatcher Institute and served on a number of committees and foundations concerned with family planning, health planning and population policy. Barbara L. Lindheim is a senior analyst at Urban Systems Research & Engineering, Inc. in Cambridge, Massachusetts. Philip R. Lee is currently professor of social medicine and director of the Health Policy Program at the School of Medicine, University of California at San Francisco. In the following viewpoint, the authors argue for legalized abortion on the grounds that it has replaced the dangerous and illegal operations of the past.

As you read, consider the following questions:

1. In what ways do the authors believe that legal abortion has improved public health?
2. How are current conditions different from those which existed when abortion was illegal, according to the author?
3. What other social conditions do the authors believe that legal abortion has improved?

There already is wide agreement that the single most important effect of legalization has been the substitution of safe, legal procedures for abortions that formerly were obtained illegally. This substitution quickly led to a dramatic decline in the number of women who died or suffered serious, sometimes permanent, injury from botched, clandestine abortions. . . .

A second, equally important result of legalization concerns *equity:* before abortion was legal, it was poor women, minority women, and very young women who suffered most, since their only options often were delivery of an unwanted child or a back-alley or self-induced abortion. . . .

By the 1960s, the illegal abortion business was flourishing. Puerto Rico and Mexico had become widely known abortion centers. Many large U.S. cities had underworld abortion rings. In some states, clergymen formed problem pregnancy consultation services that referred women to competent, though illegal, practitioners. These consultation services were used primarily by women of means, not the poor. Most illegal abortions continued to be performed under unsafe—usually degrading—conditions.

Illegal abortionists apprehended in this period following the deaths of their clients included a boatyard worker, a real-estate salesman, a hospital orderly, and an automotive mechanic. These operators often worked under unsanitary conditions and avoided anesthesia, so they could speed women who had just been aborted on their way.

As awful as illegal abortions were, the self-abortion methods that many desperate women used were even more dangerous; these included lye, soap, Lysol, and iodine douches, as well as self-inserted catheters, knitting needles, and goose quills.

No Records Kept

No records were kept of these clandestine procedures. They are known from hospital and coroners' reports on women who died from abortion complications. There were 320 such deaths recorded in 1961. This toll dropped steadily during the 1960s, as a result of advances in contraception and medical care and of the increased availability of legal abortion after 1967. By 1972, when 587,000 legal abortions were reported nationally, only 39 women died from illegal or self-induced procedures. In 1973, the year of the Supreme Court decisions, illegal abortion deaths fell to 19 and then to an average of fewer than five a year since 1974.

Information from hospitals on admissions for septic and incomplete abortion corroborate this trend. At Grady Memorial Hospital, Atlanta's large public hospital, admissions for complications of illegal abortion dropped from 33 per calendar quarter in 1970 to five in the final quarter of 1973. Between 1967 and 1970, the Los Angeles County/University of Southern California Medical

Center reported a decline of more than 50 percent in admissions due to septic abortion and a 78 percent reduction in the ratio of septic abortions to live births.

The rate of admissions for septic and incomplete abortions in New York City's municipal hospitals declined by more than 40 percent between 1969 and 1973. Before legalization, large public institutions like Harlem and Kings County hospitals reserved beds for these cases because they were so common. In about one case in four, the instrument used to induce the abortion still was present in the uterus and had to be surgically removed. Many women misplaced a catheter in the urinary bladder, rather than in the uterine cavity; these required cystoscopic removal. Septic abortion patients often were critically ill and required intensive medical and nursing care for up to a month.

Michael Keefe for the *Denver Post*, reprinted with permission.

A few years brought dramatic change. In 1976, it was reported that when a patient was admitted to a large New York municipal hospital with a diagnosis of "septic abortion," the entire resident staff was brought in to see what had become a "rare event." Only seven years earlier, 6,524 cases of septic and incomplete abortions had been admitted to municipal hospitals during the year. . . .

Death resulting from legal abortion is a very rare occurrence and easy to measure. Nonfatal complications occur more frequently but are difficult to monitor in a uniform manner. To determine the incidence of such complications, CDC conducted a four-year study in 32 hospital centers that performed more than 80,000 abortions. Morbidity was found to be influenced by length of gestation, the abortion method, the woman's race and age, and the number of children she had borne.

In the first trimester, less than half of one percent of all abortion patients experience major complications. The main risks result from delay: between the eighth and twelfth weeks, the risk of major complications doubles from two per thousand to four per thousand, while at 17 weeks, it rises to 17 per thousand. The most common complications are bleeding, infection, and injury to the cervix or uterus.

Legal Abortion Reduces Complications

Since 1973, the proportion of women obtaining abortions before the eighth week—and using the safest method, suction curettage—has steadily increased. By improving availability and accessibility, legalization thus has also contributed to a significant decline in complications.

The second major consequence of the shift from illegal to legal abortion has been to increase equity. Before legalization, there was in fact not one illegal abortion market, but two. Women with knowledge and means could usually obtain a reasonably safe abortion, performed by a physician, at a cost of $500 to $1,500, and up. For women without information and funds, this option was unavailable.

Biostatistician Christopher Tietze of the Population Council has noted that one effect of the increasing availability of safe illegal and legal abortion for middle-class American women in the 1950s and 1960s was a dramatic rise in the *differential* abortion mortality experienced by black and white women. In 1933, when abortion was generally unavailable and unsafe for all, black women suffered twice the abortion mortality reported for whites: by 1966, when safe abortions were more easily available for those who could pay, the death rate from abortion was six times greater among blacks than among whites.

A study conducted in poverty neighborhoods in New York City in the mid-1960s suggests why this was so. One woman in 12 in the sample reported an abortion attempt. Eighty percent of the women who had attempted abortion had tried to terminate the pregnancy themselves; only 2 percent said a doctor had been involved in any way! . . .

The 1973 Supreme Court abortion decisions, and subsequent diffusion of abortion services to smaller communities, have resulted in dramatic decreases in cost. A medical procedure that cost $1,500 when abortion was illegal could be obtained for $500 in a hospital soon after the Supreme Court decisions and for $150 after free-standing (nonhospital) abortion clinics were established. These changes have helped to alleviate these former inequities—but they have not eliminated them.

The increased availability of safe, legal abortions has had other positive social consequences. These more lasting effects are difficult to measure, but some conclusions can be drawn. A series of studies show how legal abortion has led to a reduction in out-of-wedlock births; many of these births are to teenagers. And the greater health risks to mother and infant resulting from early childbearing have been well documented. The social and economic costs are staggering: teenage parents are more likely to drop out of school, to have more children, and to have more births that are closely spaced, out-of-wedlock, and unwanted than those who defer childbearing until their 20s. When they marry, teenage parents are more likely to end up in the divorce courts. Because they lack education, they are less likely to hold skilled, well-paying jobs, and their incomes and savings are permanently reduced; they are more likely to depend on public welfare.

Legal Abortion: A Good Idea

If you wonder whether legal abortion is a good idea, ask any woman who survived an illegal one.

She'll tell you how painful, dirty, humiliating, and horribly dangerous a back-alley abortion was.

But despite the incredible risks, millions of American women had abortions before they were legalized nationwide in 1973. An untold number were maimed for life. Thousands were literally slaughtered, packed off bleeding and infected to die in abject terror.

Today the threat to women's lives and health no longer comes from abortion. It comes from those who want to outlaw it. People who argue that abortions should be banned—even if the result will be as horrifying as it was in the past.

Planned Parenthood Federation, advertisement, 1985.

Not only do the children of teenage parents risk greater likelihood of damage at birth, but also there is evidence that they too are likely to suffer long-lasting educational and economic deprivation. The web of negative health, social, and economic consequences associated with early childbearing suggests that the use of legal abortion by more than 400,000 teenagers annually to avoid unwanted births has benefited themselves, their children, and society.

VIEWPOINT 2

> *"The medical hazards of legally induced abortion are very significant."*

Legal Abortion Harms Public Health

Thomas W. Hilgers

Thomas W. Hilgers, M.D. is a 1969 graduate of the University of Minnesota School of Medicine. He has worked on and written a number of anti-abortion materials including an Amicus Curiae Brief to the United States Supreme Court, *Induced Abortion: A Documented Report*, written for presentation to the Minnesota State Legislature, and *Abortion and Social Justice*, an anthology from which this article is excerpted. Currently the Director of the Natural Family Planning Education and Research Center at Creighton University in Omaha, Nebraska, Dr. Hilgers is a co-founder and member of the Advisory Committee of the National Youth Pro-Life Coalition. In the following viewpoint, Dr. Hilgers argues that even though abortion has been legalized, it remains a complicated procedure that can potentially harm a woman's ability to bear normal, healthy babies in the future.

As you read, consider the following questions:

1. Why are abortion complications more frequent in young women, according to the author?
2. What are some of the complications of abortion the author cites?

The most common early complications of legally induced abortion are infection, hemorrhage, perforation of the uterus and laceration of the cervix. . . .

Stallworthy, Moolgaoker, and Walsh reported, in the prestigious British medical journal *Lancet*, . . . the complications which they noted when performing 1,182 legal abortions. While there were no deaths, 9.5% of their patients required blood transfusion, 4.2% had cervical lacerations, and in 1.2% the uterus was perforated. All of the perforations were associated with suction curettage. Emergency exploratory abdominal surgery was required for the recovery of six patients and hysterectomy was necessary for two others to save their lives. Post-abortion infection occurred in 27%.

Serious Complications

Commenting upon these complications, in the discussion which followed the presentation of their results, they said:

> The incidence of the complications described and the severity of some of them are disquieting. Some may claim that termination of pregnancy is much safer in their hands. If so, they are to be congratulated. The present figures represent the combined experience of five consultants and a series of experienced lecturers, senior registrars, and registrars. It is perhaps significant that some of the more serious complications occurred with the most senior and experienced operators. This emphasizes that termination of pregnancy is neither as simple nor as safe as some advocates of abortion-on-demand would have the public believe. . . .It is disquieting that post-abortal infection, which is one of the common causes of death after criminal abortion, should have occurred in 27% of this series. Septicemia, peritonitis, and paralytic ileus are potentially fatal complications, and the risk of death increases if they occur after the patient is discharged from the hospital and there is delay in diagnosis.

They went on to further observe:

> If termination of pregnancy were as safe as so many advocates of liberal abortion maintain, a patient suffering as a result of the operation could claim that professional negligence was responsible for her subsequent distress or disaster and plead *res ipsa loquitur.* Such claims would generally be grossly unfair. There would be great sympathy for a 16-year-old girl whose uterus was torn beyond repair; for the married woman with gut resection and peritonitis; for the mother in monthly distress following hysterotomy because of implantation endometriosis in her abdominal wall, vagina, or bladder; for the anxious infertile wife who knows that the tubal damage which now denies her the baby she desires is the delayed price she is paying for her teenage abortion. But the fact remains that none of these situations may be the result of negligence. They are complications which, though well known to, and well documented by, those with wide experience of an operation which is neither sim-

ple nor safe, are seldom mentioned by those who claim that abortion is safe and merely an extension of contraceptive techniques.

There is evidence to suggest that these complications are far more frequent in the young woman pregnant for the first time, presumably because the cervix is much more rigid in women who have not previously given birth. . . .

Hemorrhage and Infection

Infection may be localized as in endometritis, salpingitis or parametritis. It may be more regionally located resulting in pelvic thrombophlebitis, pelvic cellulitis or pelvic peritonitis. It may be distant as infection in pneumonia, endocarditis, or septic emboli to the lungs or brain. Or, the infection may be generalized as in septicemia. The infection is usually the direct result of the instrumentation involved in the abortive technique, and is the usual cause of any subsequent sterility because the infection scars the tubes to a point where they either obstruct or malfunction.

Hemorrhage is not uncommon following induced abortion even early in pregnancy. The uterus is a highly vascular organ during pregnancy because of its natural response to the life support of the child. Hemorrhage usually results when this vascular organ is lacerated, perforated, ruptured, fails to contract (uterine atony), or because of retained placental tissue. . . .

Dangers of Abortion

Deaths and near deaths do occur with every type abortion procedure. As the vast majority of abortions are done for social reasons, deaths and near deaths that do occur from the operation are especially tragic.

All members of the medical profession, abortion counselors and social workers should be kept apprised of the diversity of dangers inherent in the abortion procedure. A plea is made for the accurate reporting of all legal abortion deaths and near deaths.

Matthew J. Bulfin, paper presented before the American College of Obstetricians and Gynecologists, October 28, 1975.

Perforation of the uterus occurs in 1.0-2.0% of legally induced abortions, and may occur with the traditional D&C or the newer method of suction curettage. Perforation occurs primarily because the surgeon operates by "touch" alone, and not under direct vision. Secondarily, the pregnant uterus is much softer than the nonpregnant uterus, lending itself to easy perforation. If, in the process of perforation, the bowel or a blood vessel is torn, overwhelming infection and/or hemorrhage may occur, necessitating exploratory laparotomy. . . .

Early physical complications which are very significant when they occur, but are less frequent, include the following:

1. Coma and/or convulsions because of the effects on the central nervous system and/or kidneys of hypertonic saline entering the bloodstream directly or via the peritoneal cavity.
2. Embolisation of air, most commonly, or by particulate matter (fat, placental products, amniotic fluid) in the heart, pulmonary artery, brain and other organs.
3. Anesthetic accidents resulting in cardiac arrest or aspiration pneumonia.
4. Disturbances in the coagulability of the maternal blood. In fact, a mild form of consumption coagulopathy is very common with saline abortion (manifest by hypofibrinogenemia and thrombocytopenia).
5. The abortion of only one twin while the other survives and delivers normally several months later. The psychological effect on the mother and the surviving twin in such cases has not been investigated.
6. It is now becoming apparent that, contrary to wishful thinking, abortion can be a relatively uncomfortable procedure. For early abortion many patients can be managed adequately with mild sedation and paracervical local anesthesia, but for a "considerable" number this is not sufficient to provide satisfactory analgesia, nor to prevent agitated and abrupt pelvic movements which can only contribute to increasing the complication rate. . . .

Complications in Subsequent Pregnancies

Subsequent pregnancies are more often pathological following legal abortion, and this, it seems to me, represents some of the most significant complications of all. Any one of these could produce an individual disaster at least equivalent to any unwanted pregnancy and one which may be far more difficult to handle.

The prematurity rate in Hungary in 1954 (before legalized abortion) was 7%. However, in 1968 (14 years after legalization) it had increased to 12%. The incidence of prematurity developing in any one individual has been shown to be well correlated with the number of abortions a woman has. . . . The increase in prematurity is thought to be a direct result of the instrumentation required in early abortion; dilating the cervix may leave the cervix incompetent to retain the child for the full nine months. . . .

A number of countries have reported a significant increase in the incidence of ectopic pregnancy. One Japanese study revealed that 3.9% of women with previous history of legal abortion had a subsequent ectopic pregnancy. This is eight times the incidence of ectopic pregnancy in the United States. An ectopic pregnancy, of course, is not infrequently life-threatening because of rupture and hemorrhage. This, therefore, subjects an individual woman to a very substantial future risk. The risk of death from ectopic pregnancy in the United States is approximately 300/100,000. Again, tubal malfunction, usually secondary to post-abortal infection, seems to be the prime cause.

The incidence of spontaneous abortion in women with a history of previous legal abortion is reported to be 30-40% higher than in those without such a history and the incidence of fetal death during pregnancy is twice as great. Also, complicated labors (prolonged labor, placenta previa, adherent placenta) and excessive bleeding at the time of delivery have all been noted to occur more commonly in subsequent pregnancies to women with a previous history of legal abortion. These, of course, all result in increased obstetrical intervention. . . .

Significant Medical Hazards

The medical hazards of legally induced abortion are very significant and should be conscientiously weighed to obtain a balanced and ethical viewpoint. Singling out only one set of "facts" or figures to serve as evidence to safety cannot occasion this end. Abortion must be recognized for what it is: a morbid invasion of a *healthy* woman's body with the purpose of destroying new life. One wonders what pressures in our modern society have brought about so radical a change in moral climate that powerful groups of physicians feel compelled to mislead the public regarding this danger-fraught reality.

3 VIEWPOINT

"The control . . . women sought through abortion was a meaningful one given the changing context of their lives."

Legal Abortion Strengthens Women's Rights

Kristin Luker

Many people who support legal abortion argue that it is women's constitutional right. The ability to choose when to have a child aided women in their marital and sexual freedom, and their choice of careers. In the following viewpoint, excerpted from her latest book, *Abortion and the Politics of Motherhood*, Kristin Luker supports these views. She argues that the increased involvement of women in the workplace made abortion on demand a necessity. Ms. Luker is an associate professor of sociology at the University of California, San Diego.

As you read, consider the following questions:

1. Why does the author believe that abortion laws were necessary for women to achieve equal job opportunities?
2. Why does the author believe that abortion laws are necessary to end job discrimination?

The mobilization of significant numbers of women around the issue of abortion laws can. . .be seen as an attack on a symbolic linch-pin that held together a complicated set of assumptions about who women were, what their roles in life should be, what kinds of jobs they should take in the paid labor force, and how those jobs should be rewarded. "Equal pay for equal work" was already a revolutionary demand in this context, but until women could get equal work, even this demand was irrelevant. And women could not get equal work until they could challenge the assumption that their work activities were, or ought to be, or might be subordinated to family plans. Since significant numbers of women were *already* combining work and family, the idea that they should pay a large economic penalty for being women with family obligations came to seem fundamentally unfair.

It is in this context that we can understand what women activists mean when they claimed that they had a *right* to their own bodies. As they came to expect to work much or most of their adult lives, just as men did, an unplanned pregnancy came to be seen as a tragedy. And for men, or the state, or physicians to have control over whether pregnancy would take place—and for women to suffer alone the consequences that decision would have for their careers, or education, or social status—came to seem eminently wrong and cruelly oppressive.

Women's Control Over Their Lives

When women accepted the definition that a woman's primary role was as wife and mother, control of one's own body meant little. When the biological workings of one's body and one's social status (or intended social status) are congruent, who needs control? In everyday terms, if one's role in life is to be a mother, it is not such a problem that one's biology often seems singlemindedly bent on producing children. But when some groups of women began to think of themselves as having a different primary role in life, the brute facts of biology came to seem at odds with how they saw themselves. Once they had choices about life roles, they came to feel that they had *a right to use abortion in order to control their own lives.*

Thus one activist said:

> If I hadn't had that abortion early in my life, my life would have been a disaster. I never would have gotten to medical school. I was married at that point to a very ill man, and it would have just been terrible to have a baby. So many times I've heard similar stories from people. I mean, people who need abortions are frequently in some sort of turmoil, and it's really a life-saving thing for many people. . . .Women are manipulated to have babies or not have babies by the needs of the state, and I have a lot of pent-up emotion about that.

Another woman, a reformer (who still subscribes to the remnants of physician control over abortion), articulated the same theme:

> For women to achieve any kind of equality in the employment market requires acceptance by society that they are in control of their reproductive lives. . . .Legalized abortion, the right of every women to have an abortion, given a reason that her doctor concurs with, is certainly a factor in freeing women from the blanket accusation that they're going to be divided in their loyalty to their career because they're going to have children. I think they're free to have children anyway, but I think the attitude is different to some extent.

Making Abortion Illegal Won't End It

If a woman's choice about whether or not to bear a child—one of the most personal choices a woman can make—can be determined by others, then how can we make the case for women's rights in general? Then where do we stand on equal opportunity in the workplace, equal pay for equal work, even the opportunity to pursue our individual talents and our dreams? . . .

I have never forgotten that I was forced to resort to something illegal to implement something so very personal. I am determined that neither my children nor any women regardless of age or economic status will have to endure such a humiliating, degrading experience because there is no other option.

Abortion made illegal will not stop abortions. It would just recreate a black market for illegal abortions.

Carolyn Buhl, *USA Today*, November 23, 1984.

One of the earliest activists in favor of repeal made the point most directly:

> I started in 1963. I was interested in doing a book for young women, perhaps sophomores in high school. I wanted to explain to them what I could see, and what everyone else our age can see—that they would not live the ideal dream life of getting married and having the house with the fence around it and the two or three children and the man who would take care of them forever. I wanted to [urge them to] finish their education and prepare themselves to take care of themselves, by work or whatever. . . .I know that most young women will have to work sometime during their lives, and I felt that a little book slanted toward them at this time in their lives might be more effective in making them understand [this]. . . . Anyhow, when I researched this business of how we could prepare young women—in other words, even get a scholarship for young women—we were blocked at every turn. . . . They would say, "Oh, she's only going to get married and have babies."

A happily married Catholic woman with a small child, who

joined the movement in 1970, is typical of how the message of rights was heard by the wider public after 1967. Unlike earlier activists, she never had any direct experience with abortion (although she did distress her conservative Catholic family by using birth control), but as a working woman the message of the movement made sense to her. (Note incidentally the point at which she unconsciously switches from using the term "they" to "we" when speaking of women.)

> I went to this meeting where women spoke about having children. I had a lot of thoughts about the role of having children, about how having children should be your choice. I was trying to figure out how women got into the position they were in, and what were some of the main points that kept women in what I think was a very bad situation—by themselves, isolated, in these little house with their children, with no educational opportunities, no jobs. And a lot of it seemed to me to focus around the having children aspect of it—having children at times when they weren't prepared to have them, in the middle of going to school, whatever. And maybe abortion was just one more aspect of that. [I was] beginning to think that if we actually decided ourselves when and where we were going to have children, that would be a big step toward taking some kind of charge. . . .

The Demand to Repeal All Laws

The demand for repeal of all abortion laws was an attack on both the segregated labor market and the cultural expectations about women's roles. It allowed women to argue (and symbolically demonstrate) that although childbearing was important, it was not the single most important thing in a woman's life. And by asserting the right of women to control fertility, it vitiated the arguments of employers that only certain jobs were "good for a woman." Once women obtained control of their fertility, it would become clear that the labor market discriminated against them simply because they were women. In a society that had recently experienced a nationwide upheaval over civil rights, such discrimination would be difficult to justify. With the control over fertility in their own hands, even this ground would be disqualified. . . .

Women Needed Control Over Fertility

In the twentieth century the value of children as economic producers in the family continued to be low, and the forces that made children economically "costly"—their exclusion from the labor market and the extension of compulsory schooling—continued to expand. If the first abortion controversy was a reaction to the declining economic value of large families to nineteenth-century Americans, then the second abortion controversy can be seen as a reaction to the increasing economic cost of children to *women* in the twentieth century. When women wanted control of their own bodies, they wanted control over the number and, more important, the timing of their births because an untimely or unintended birth (or even the threat of one) could have dramatic consequences for their lives.

The control. . .women sought through abortion was a meaningful one given the changing context of their lives. Their concerns, when combined with the desire of physicians to perform the kinds of abortions they had traditionally done, free of "religious" or "outside" interference, grew into a compelling social movement. It was so compelling, in fact, that the U.S. Supreme Court agreed to hear arguments about the legality of nineteenth-century abortion laws in general. After hearing arguments for both sides, the Court found all abortion laws unconstitutionally vague.

4 VIEWPOINT

"Of all the things which are done to women to fit them into a society dominated by men, abortion is the most violent invasion of their physical and psychic integrity."

Legal Abortion Exploits Women

Daphne de Jong

Daphne de Jong is the president of Feminists for Life, a New Zealand organization. In the following viewpoint, Ms. de Jong claims that legal abortion has destroyed, rather than helped, women's rights. Instead of demanding the right to destroy their unborn babies, women should fight for the right to have those babies. Only when women insist that their essential role as mothers be recognized both in their private lives and in the workplace, will they achieve full equality.

As you read, consider the following questions:

1. What reasons does the author give for her argument that legal abortion manipulates and degrades women?
2. How does the author criticize the idea that abortion is a necessity?
3. How does abortion infringe on the rights of others, according to the author?

Daphne de Jong, "The Feminist Sell-Out," *New Zealand Listener*, January 14, 1976.
Reprinted with permission.

The women's movement suffers from three classic defense mechanisms associated with minority group status: self-rejection, identification with the dominant group, and displacement.

The demand for abortion at will is a symptom of group self-hatred and total rejection, not of sex *role* but of sex identity.

The womb is not the be-all and end-all of woman's existence. But it is the physical centre of her sexual identity, which is an important aspect of her self-image and personality. To reject its function, or to regard it as a handicap, a danger or a nuisance, is to reject a vital part of her own personhood. Every woman need not be a mother, but unless every woman can identify with the potential motherhood of all women, no equality is possible. American Negroes gained nothing by straightening their kinky hair and aping the white middle class. Equality began to become a reality only when they insisted on acceptance of their different qualities—"Black is Beautiful."

Pregnant Peoples' Rights

Women will gain their rights only when they demand recognition of the fact that they are people who become pregnant and give birth—and not always at infallibly convenient times—and that pregnant people have the same rights as others.

To say that in order to be equal with men it must be possible for a pregnant woman to become unpregnant at will, is to say that being a woman precludes her from being a fully functioning person. It concedes the point to those who claim that women who want equality really want to be imitation men.

If women must submit to abortion to preserve their lifestyle or career, their economic or social status, they are pandering to a system devised and run by men for male convenience. The politics of sexism are perpetuated by accommodating to expediential societal structures which decree that pregnancy is incompatible with other activities, and that children are the sole responsibility of their mother.

The demand for abortion is a sell-out to male values and a capitulation to male lifestyles rather than a radical attempt to renegotiate the terms by which women and men can live in the world as people with equal rights and equal opportunities. Black "Uncle Toms" have their counterparts not only in women who cling to the chains of their kitchen sinks, but also in those who proclaim their own liberation while failing to recognize that they have merely adopted the standards of the oppressor, and fashioned themselves in his image.

Oppressed groups traditionally turn their frustrated vengeance on those even weaker than themselves. The unborn is the natural scapegoat for the repressed anger and hostility of women, which is denied in traditional male-female relationships, and ridiculed when it manifests itself in feminist protest. Even while proclaiming "her" rights over the fetus, much liberationist rhetoric identifies pregnancy with male chauvinst "ownership." The inference is that by implanting "his" seed, the man establishes some claim over a woman's body ("Keeping her barefoot and pregnant"). Abortion is almost consciously seen as "getting back at" the male. The truth may well be that the liberationist sees the fetus not as a part of her body but as a part of his.

Abortion Manipulates Women

What escapes most liberationist writers is that legal abortion is neither a remedy nor an atonement for male exploitation of women. It is merely another way in which women are manipulated and degraded for male convenience and male profit. This becomes blantantly obvious in the private abortion industries of both Britain and America, and the support given to the pro-abortion lobby by such exploitative corporations as the *Playboy* empire.

Dana Summers, *The Orlando Sentinel*, reprinted with permission.

Of all the things which are done to women to fit them into a society dominated by men, abortion is the most violent invasion of their physical and psychic integrity. It is a deeper and more destructive assault than rape, the culminating act of womb-envy and woman-hatred by the jealous male who resents the creative power of women.

Just as the rapist claims to be "giving women what they want," the abortionist affirms his right to provide a service for which there is a feminine demand.

Offered the quick expedient of abortion, instead of community support to allow her to experience pregnancy and birth and parenthood with dignity and without surrendering her rights as a person, woman is again the victim, and again a willing participant in her own destruction.

The way to equality is not to force women into molds designed for men, but to re-examine our basic assumptions about men and women, about child-care and employment, about families and society, and design new and more flexible modes for living. Accepting short-term solutions like abortion only delays the implementation of real reforms like decent maternity and paternity leaves, job protection, high quality child-care, community responsibility for dependent people of all ages, and recognititon of the economic contribution of child-minders. Agitation for the imaginative use of glide time, shared jobs, shorter working weeks, good creches, part-time education and job training, is more constructive for women—and men—torn between career and children, than agitation for abortion.

Women Processed Through Abortion Mills

Today's women's movement remains rooted in 19th-century thinking, blindly accepting patriarchal systems as though they rested on some immutable natural law; processing women through abortion mills to manufacture instant imitation men who will fit into a society made by and for wombless people. Accepting the "necessity" of abortion is accepting that pregnant women and mothers are unable to function as persons in this society. It indicates a willingness to adjust to the status quo which is a betrayal of the feminist cause, a loss of the revolutionary vision of a world fit for *people* to live in.

The movement has never perceived the essential disharmony of its views on sexual oppression and its aspirations to a new social order, and its attitudes to abortion. The accepted feminist prophets of the new age have never brought to bear on the question the analytical power which they display in other directions. Typically the subject is dismissed in a paragraph or two, the "right" to abortion assumed, without evidence or argument. (Simone de Beauvoir came closest to recognizing the dangers, raging that women were often coerced into abortions they did not truly want— by men or by the circumstances of the pregnancy.)

Within the movement, doctors and other men whose attitudes are glaringly chauvinist have been hailed as white knights of women's rights if they espouse abortion on demand, while "sisters" who oppose it are subjected to witch-hunts that could teach a thing or two to a Sprenger or a McCarthy.

The reasons for the abortion issue moving to a central position in liberation ideology are partly tactical. It is much easier to fight a statute than to overcome social attitudes. As the suffragette movement became cohesive and powerful by focusing attention on the single issue of the vote, the new feminist wave gained momentum when all its resources were thrown into overturning abortion laws.

But the vote was dismissed by some feminists of the 1960s as "the red herring of the revolution." The abortion issue bids fair to be its successor. . . .

Human rights are not exclusive. Any claim to a superior or exceptional right inevitably infringes on the rights of someone else. To ignore the rights of others in an effort to assert our own is to compound injustice, rather than reduce it.

a critical thinking skill

Distinguishing Primary from Secondary Sources

A critical thinker must always question sources of information. Historians, for example, usually distinguish between *primary sources* (a firsthand or eyewitness account from personal letters, documents, or speeches, etc.) and *secondary sources* (a "second-hand" account usually based upon a "firsthand" account and possibly appearing in newspapers, encyclopedias, or other similar types of publications). A woman's account of her botched, illegal abortion is an example of a primary source. A history of abortion that includes a portion of this woman's account would be an example of a secondary source.

It must be noted that interpretation and/or point of view also play a role when dealing with primary and secondary sources. For example, the historian writing about the abortion issue not only will quote the woman's account but also will interpret it. It is certainly a possibility that his or her interpretation may be incorrect. Even the diary or primary source must be questioned as to interpretation and point of view. The woman may have been a pro-choice activist who exaggerated her experience to stress the need for legal abortion.

This activity is designed to test your skill in evaluating sources of information. Pretend that your teacher tells you to write a research report on the effects of legal abortion on public health. You decide to include an equal number of primary and secondary sources. Listed below are a number of sources which may be useful in your research. Carefully evaluate each of them. Then, *place a P next to those descriptions you believe are primary sources.* Second, *rank the primary sources* assigning the number (1) to what appears to be the most objective and accurate primary source, the number (2) to the next most objective, and so on until the ranking is finished. *Repeat the entire procedure, this time placing an S next to those descriptions you feel would serve as secondary sources and then ranking them.*

If you are doing this activity as a member of a class or group, discuss and compare your evaluation with other members of the group. If you are reading this book alone you may want to ask others if they agree with your evaluation. Either way, you will find the interaction valuable.

P or S		*Rank in Importance*
______	1. an article written by a woman who recounts her severe depression following her legal abortion	______
______	2. research published in a medical journal comparing abortion-related death statistics before and after legal abortion and concluding legal abortion has improved public health	______
______	3. an editorial opposing legal abortion written by a woman who decided against having an abortion	______
______	4. a research paper by a prominent psychologist explaining why legal abortion has helped women	______
______	5. a TV documentary interviewing women about their abortions prior to the legalization of abortion	______
______	6. a published interview with a doctor who performed abortions before legalization	______
______	7. a history of the abortion issue published in 1985	______
______	8. the Supreme Court's opinion delivered in 1973 making abortion legal	______
______	9. an editorial published after the 1973 Supreme Court decision supporting legal abortion	______
______	10. a poem by a prominent feminist detailing the horrors committed by "back-alley butchers"	______
______	11. an article in *Newsweek* on the pro-life movement's push to make abortion illegal	______
______	12. an interview with a pro-life activist on the need to make abortion illegal	______

Periodical Bibliography

The following list of periodical articles deals with the subject matter of this chapter.

James A. Brix	"Looking Past Abortion Rhetoric," *The Christian Century*, October 24, 1984.
David R. Carlin Jr.	"Abortion, Religion and the Law," *America*, December 1, 1984.
Kay Castonguay	"Pro-Life and Feminist? Being Both Is Possible!" *Catholic Bulletin Magazine*, June 2/8, 1985.
Christianity Today	"Within Our Reach: A Building Consensus Could at Least Put an End to Abortion on Demand," *Christianity Today*, April 19, 1985.
Paige Comstock Cunningham	"Reversing Roe vs. Wade," *Christianity Today*, September 20, 1985.
Ellen Goodman	"Anti-Abortion Folks Have the Big Mo—Blame the Media," *Los Angeles Times*, February 1, 1985.
Beverly Wildung Harrison	"Abortion Has Made a Difference in the Lives of Women! " *Engage/Social Action*, March 1983.
Newsweek	"America's Abortion Dilemma," January 14, 1985.
John T. Noonan Jr.	"Knee-Jerk Spasms on Roe vs. Wade," *Los Angeles Times*, August 8, 1985.
Origins	"Abortion and the Law Today: Administration's Brief," September 19, 1985.
Policy Review	"Split Verdict: What Americans Think About Abortion," Spring 1985.
The Progressive	"The Wire Next Time?" April 15, 1985.
Revolutionary Worker	"'Silent No More' Testimony, No Going Back to the Back Alley," June 10, 1985.
George Scialabba	"The Trouble with 'Roe' v. 'Wade,'" *Village Voice*, July 16, 1985.
Libby Smith	"I'm a Criminal and Proud of It: An Abortion Outlaw Speaks Up," *Mademoiselle*, August 1982.

CHAPTER 6

Are Extremist Tactics Justified in the Abortion Debate?

1 VIEWPOINT

"What the abortionists are doing is evil. Out of love, we do what we must to change their minds."

Pro-Life Extremist Tactics Are Necessary

Joseph M. Scheidler

A graduate of Notre Dame and Marquette Universities, Joseph Scheidler has worked for a number of newspapers and magazines, including the *South Bend Tribune.* Formerly the executive director of the Illinois Right to Life Committee and the head of Friends for Life, he is presently the director of the Pro-Life Action League in Chicago. Although it has only three full-time staff people, the Pro-Life Action League has become one of the most visible and widely publicized pro-life organizations in America. Mr. Scheidler's controversial tactics have greatly contributed to this visibility. These tactics—he regularly recommends harassing abortion clinic patrons, using gory photos to shock and appall people, and open deception to end abortion, echo those of an Old Testament prophet railing against an indifferent public. In the following viewpoint, excerpted from his book, *Closed: 99 Ways to Stop Abortion*, Mr. Scheidler explains that these tactics are harsh, but necessary, to make people realize the horror of abortion.

As you read, consider the following questions:

1. What is the author's primary feeling for the people he opposes?
2. What is the basis of the pro-life movement, according to the author?

Joseph M. Scheidler, *Closed: 99 Ways to Stop Abortion*. Lake Bluff, Illinois: Regnery Books, 1985. Used by permission of Regnery Gateway, Inc., 950 North Shore Drive, Lake Bluff, Illinois 60044, (312) 440-1647. Contact Regnery Gateway for special discounts to pro-life groups.

Even though some of the things pro-life activists do to stop abortion may seem hostile, we must never lose sight of the fact that what we are trying to do is save lives, while helping preserve women's mental, physical, and spiritual health. We can do these things only if we love the people we confront.

Our concern is manifest in what Fr. John Powell, S.J. calls "tough love." It is not soft, saccharine love, but a love that says, "We want you to do the right thing. But since you don't know what is right, we will make you look at abortion in its ugly reality. If you can't learn through persuasion, we will use pressure." That doesn't mean we don't love the abortionists. The parent who never punishes an unruly child doesn't love his child. A weak parent is concerned about being liked and fails to do the loving thing. What we are doing has to be done, like punishing an unruly child. What the abortionists are doing is evil. Out of love, we do what we must to change their minds.

Punishment Is a Necessity

Franky Schaeffer told pro-lifers that the most loving thing he had done in the past year was to spank his son, who had run into the street and nearly got hit by a truck. To prevent future tragedy, punishment had to be administered. Punishment might save his son's life. It was given because Franky Schaeffer loves his son and wants him around for a few more years.

Those of us who confront the abortionists and debate them on radio and television, do not like them very much. They are selfish and humorless. But occasionally one is likeable, and you feel a genuine concern for him. Sometimes it is hard to realize that to make a living, he kills children and ruins women's lives.

But whatever natural revulsion or even attraction they elicit, the fact remains that everything we do in relation to the abortionists is done because we love them. We do not want anyone to lose his soul. We do not want the abortionists to be punished in hell for eternity. Yet we believe there is reward and punishment after this life, that good will be rewarded and evil punished. Our determination to get the abortionists out of their grizzly business is a greater act of love than they are shown by their colleagues.

To talk a person out of doing abortions or to put him out of business shows greater love than excusing what he does. We tell abortionists that what they do is wrong. Who loved Herod? John the Baptist, who pointed out his evil and told him to repent, or Herodias, who asked for the head of John? John tried to convert Herod. Herodias merely wanted the Baptist silenced. Throughout history, it has been those who really love who try to convert people from evil to good.

We know in advance that love for our enemy will be

misconstrued and that we will be made fun of for mentioning it. Many cannot understand what we are talking about. Most of them will not believe us. But some suspect that we may be right. One abortion clinic operator told us she realized that what she was doing would send her to hell, but that was her decision to make and not ours. She was right. But we had to try.

For Their Good

We don't expect most abortionists to understand that what we are trying to do is for their good. It is not important that they understand.

We must be careful not to do any of these things out of hatred. We cannot fight the battle for the unborn with hatred. We do it selflessly for someone who will never know we did it. We do it knowing that the person we save at the clinic door may never realize he was in mortal danger. We do it to bear witness to society, and to the abortionists, that there is a better way to solve problems than by killing children.

Pro-life is a movement based on the highest form of altruism, so there is no room for hatred. We can hate abortion, but we cannot hate the abortionists or we betray our cause. We do everything for the love of God and the children. We are trying to save the parents who, under different circumstances, would not consider

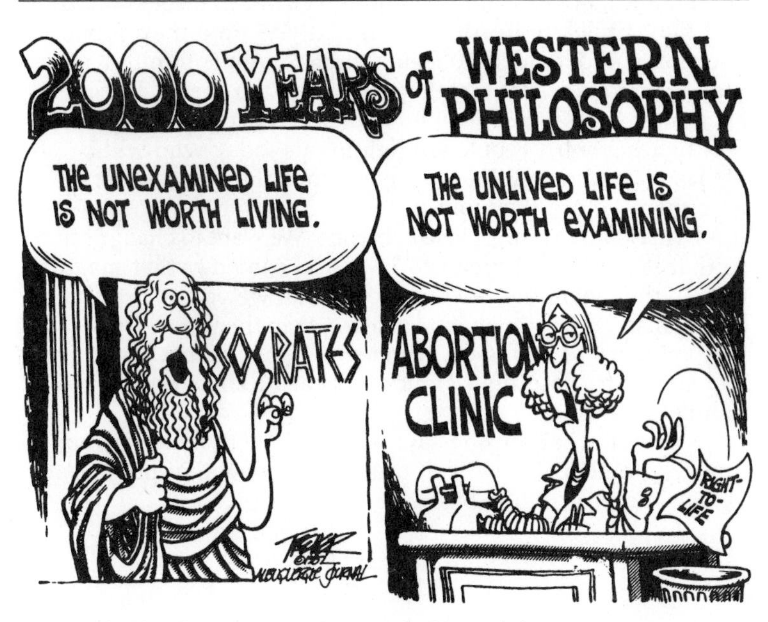

John Trever, *The Albuquerque Journal*, reprinted with permission.

abortion. We do it even out of love for the abortion providers, some of whom have been deceived into thinking they are solving a problem. Some may belief that abortion is the lesser of two evils. It is difficult to understand such a deception, but we are not in a position to judge their guilt.

We can base our activities on our hatred of abortion, but not on hatred of the abortionists. Scripture admonishes us to love our enemies and do good to those who hate us. We are told that charity is the greatest virtue and that God loves each of us. If God loves the abortionists, we must love them, too.

The ultimate hatred is that which sends a soul to hell. In *Hamlet*, the prince in planning to murder his step-father, catches him in prayer and decides not to kill him then, because he might send him to heaven. Hamlet wants his step-father to go to hell and decides to murder him in the midst of some debauchery. It is true hatred to wish to see a person eternally lost.

We Want Conversion

This is not what we want. We want the abortionists to be converted, returned to God, and be saved. We bring them to God by loving them, not by hating them.

Many women who have had abortions have repented and are now pro-lifers. Many former supporters of abortion now defend the unborn. A young Chicago couple, Darryl and Debbie Trulson, go to clinics, appear on radio and television to discuss abortion, and fight tirelessly for the unborn. At one time they supported abortion and defended it. Seeing them totally committed to pro-life, it is hard to realize that they were once the enemy. I frequently encounter pro-life people who confess, "Last year at this time I was fighting you." People are fighting us today who will be pro-life leaders tomorrow. We love them when they join us. We should love them before they join us.

As Christians, we must love everyone. We want to change society so that it is not so difficult to love, and someday that may happen. In the meantime, we must love what we've got, pray for the abortionists and, through "tough love", help them realize that what they are doing offends God. Never stop believing that your prayers and efforts to close their clinics will turn them from the evil of killing children.

No matter what anyone says about our activities, and our attitudes, whether it is evident or not, we know that pro-life nonviolent direct action is based on love.

VIEWPOINT

2

"Antichoice extremism clarifies the meaning of the right-to-life movement. . . . Here the movement is shown for what it is—not an attempt to save life, but a determination to control women's lives."

Pro-Life Extremist Tactics Should be Condemned

Lisa Cronin Wohl

In the cause of saving the unborn, the extremist side of the pro-life movement resorts to what many people would consider grisly and objectionable tactics. Harassing women both inside and outside abortion clinics, carrying bloody dolls and fetuses in jars, are just some of the methods used by anti-abortionist extremists to make their point. In the following viewpoint, Lisa Cronin Wohl argues that these tactics are appalling and unjustified. The real conclusion one must draw from these actions is that the pro-lifers wish to control women's lives. Ms. Wohl is a contributing editor to *Ms.* magazine.

As you read, consider the following questions:

1. Does the author believe the pro-life movement is more effective than the pro-choice movement? Why or why not?
2. Does the author think that the pro-life group is primarily nonviolent?
3. Why does the author believe the pro-life groups are really just sexists?

Lisa Cronin Wohl, "Antiabortion Violence on the Rise: How Far Will It Go?" *Ms.*, October 1984. Reprinted with the author's permission.

Picture yourself as a woman who has made the difficult decision to terminate a pregnancy. Like most people facing a medical procedure, you are somewhat apprehensive.

As you approach the clinic or doctor's office, you are accosted. A stranger, a self-designated "sidewalk counselor," thrusts an antichoice pamphlet at you and mutters a demand that you change your mind. If you're lucky, that's all you encounter. If your "counselors" are more extreme, you may be confronted with garbage cans full of red paint-spattered dolls representing fetuses. A full line of picketers may bar the entrance to the clinic door, screaming "murderer" at you as you try to go in.

You could be confronted with a baby doll nailed to a cross, or yelled at by someone with a megaphone. Someone may pray the rosary loudly or someone may throw "holy" water at you or follow you to the clinic door with a tape recording of a crying baby. Someone may photograph you or conspicuously take down the license number of your car. Someone will almost surely thrust pictures of bloody, mangled fetuses in your face.

Intrusive, Intimate Questions

If your "counselor" is truly aggressive, he or she may try to physically block your path. This stranger may ask intrusive, intimate questions. "Are you pregnant? Are you married? Have you had an abortion before? Do you profess any particular religion?" Then, as quickly as possible, for you are probably trying to get away by now, your "counselor" will assault you with lies and distortions about the abortion procedure, all intended to terrify you.

Who are these people? Why are they attacking you and other women who seek to exercise their right to abortion? They are the antichoice radicals who are attacking at the street level because they are losing the fight against abortion on almost every other front. Some fanatics go even further, moving secretly to destroy abortion facilities. As Alice Wolfson of the Committee To Defend Reproductive Rights, puts it, "If they can't make abortion illegal, they're going to try to make it impossible."

[On] July 4, [1983] while Washington, D.C., was still celebrating the nation's independence with fireworks, someone pumped propane gas into the kitchen area of the town house headquarters of the National Abortion Federation (NAF), a national organization of abortion providers. Around midnight, the gas, ignited by a stove's pilot light, caused an explosion that blew out windows and left the building structurally damaged.

A half hour later, not long after some NAF staffers returned to the building, they were hurriedly evacuated by police. A bomb had been found, a pipe bomb capable of flattening the town house and damaging its adjoining neighbors, had it been detonated by the propane explosion. If it had gone off with the NAF staffers and police in the building, 8 people could have been killed, and some 40 or 50 July 4 celebrants at a nearby park might have been injured. "They're going to hurt somebody," says NAF executive director Barbara Radford. "It's bound to happen."

It almost happened three days later on July 7 when someone bombed a Planned Parenthood clinic in Annapolis, Maryland, at 1:35 A.M. The clinic shares a building with several other companies, and two Air Cargo employees were working through the night when the bomb went off. They were not injured, but police say they could have been. And anyone walking near the clinic could also have been hurt. The force of the blast was strong enough to drive shrapnel through the steel sides of a pickup truck parked 150 yards away.

Respect Majority Opinion

The wave of bombings, arson and other violent attacks against reproductive health clinics is the result of a terrifying phenomenon—intolerance. . . .

In a country that relies on democracy as its basis for governance, the majority opinion must be respected, even by those who disagree.

Faye Wattleton, *USA Today*, November 23, 1984.

Of course, there has always been some picketing against abortion clinics and occasionally violent action. More than three dozen abortion facilities across the country have been hit with arson attacks since abortion was legalized in 1973, and some abortion providers have been subject to vicious, ongoing harassment. But these latest attacks represent a new level of danger. It was only by chance that the bombers and arsonists did not become murderers. . . .

More Radical Thinking

Elasah Drogin, president of the antichoice activist group Catholics United for Life (CUL), says that "People with the stick-to-itiveness to be involved with a movement like this for ten years are getting a little impatient with the National Right to Life. They want to see more happen. They want more activity. . .more radical thinking.". . .

The basic strategy of most of these groups is twofold. First through what they call "sidewalk counseling," they try to convince women—who are literally on their way into the doctor's office—to change their minds about abortion decisions. Second, they intimidate those who provide abortion services in order to force them out of the field.

"Some of them are profoundly fanatical people," charges Uta

Landy, former executive director of NAF. But how far will they go? The right-to-life movement, whether mainstream or more radical, insists it is nonviolent. "If you are truly prolife you are nonviolent," says Michael Gaworski of PEACE, [People Expressing Concern for Everyone]. "But I'm not a pacifist. I'm a nonviolent activist."

But violence happens. The fire bombings, vandalized clinics, slashed tires, crosses on an abortion staffer's front lawn, midnight phone calls that threaten injury and death—these too-common events in the antichoice war are disclaimed by movement groups. They are presented by the groups discussed here as isolated acts by unknown individuals who have no connection to the right-to-life movement as a whole.

Meaning of Nonviolence Varies

But the meaning of nonviolent activism varies from group to group. For some the limit is nonviolent picketing, an action that the prochoice movement recognizes as a legitimate First Amendment right. Other more aggressive groups say they are nonviolent, but claim a civil disobedience right to law-breaking activities such as trespassing. Their justification is the inventive legal "doctrine of necessity," the notion that you can break one law in order to obey a higher law.

"I'll sit in a clinic, there's no question about that," says Joseph Scheidler. "I'll bar the entrance. It's illegal. It's a form of trespass. But I feel exactly the way a fireman [feels] if he saw a burning building and saw people screaming upstairs. . . . You have a higher law and that is the law of necessity." . . .

The Essence of Evil

Compounding this tendency to justify lawbreaking is the antichoice extremists' characterization of the prochoice movement as the very essence of evil. Joseph Scheidler and the extremists claim that abortion is the American Holocaust, the equivalent of the Nazi Holocaust. The irony is that Hitler was antichoice: he outlawed abortion in Nazi Germany and one of the key goals of the Third Reich was to force Aryan women to have as many children as possible.

But, ignoring historical accuracy, the antichoice extremists label abortion clinics "abortuaries" and "death chambers." Scheidler calls abortion clinic workers "S.S. guards."

This, obviously, is inflammatory language. Anyone who seriously believes that abortion is mass murder—the mass murder of children—might well feel compelled to take more direct, possibly even violent, action against a clinic to stop it.

Certainly, Scheidler is left talking out of both sides of his mouth. On the one hand, he says he's against violence; on the other, he says, "violence is permissible as a last resort when it must be used to prevent or stop a greater violence." The Chicago *Sun-Times* has quoted him as telling followers, "You can try for fifty years to do it the nice polite way, or you can do it next week the nasty way. . . ."

He tells the story of a father who had beaten his own children to death, using "a hammer and an ax and a baseball bat and whatever it took. They couldn't tell if they were boys or girls he beat them up so badly." Then he adds that he sees "no difference" between that sort of murder and abortion.

Reprinted with permission.

If Scheidler and his allies really believe that stopping abortion is the same as stopping child murders, the question arises, why aren't they *more* violent? It is this question that could tilt the movement toward violence no matter how loudly its leaders proclaim their commitment to nonviolent action. Surely, they share some responsibility for those antichoice true believers who choose vigilante action in the night. . . .

Failure to Condemn Violence

Can the antichoice leaders really claim no responsibility for violence when they fail to condemn it and when their rhetoric can be seen to subtly encourage it? Or must we see the current wave of violence as part of a continuum that begins with simple picketing and goes on to catastrophe? Certainly that pattern of escalating attack is the experience of many clinics. The Everett, Washington, Feminist Health Center, for example, was picketed regularly beginning two days before it opened on August 9, 1983. The picketing started weekly and then became daily. On opening day, picketers had placed huge signs depicting bloody fetuses in the clinic windows. One woman carried a tape recording of what she said was a fetal heartbeat and played it loudly as she trailed patients into the clinic. . . .

Psychological Violence

Usually vandalism and arson occur at night and the perpetrators are rarely caught. But the other kind of violence, violence to the truth in order to undermine the psychological health of abortion clients, is easy to document. The "facts" that Scheidler uses to "counsel" women entering abortion facilities include: "About ten percent of women become sterile after one legal abortion. Tubal pregnancies, miscarriages, and premature births of your future babies are greatly increased because of an abortion. Also there is an increase in deformed babies after a woman has had an abortion." . . .

As we all know, one of the great boons of legalized abortion has been a dramatic reduction in the complications and death rates among women terminating their pregnancies. A review of more than 150 studies worldwide on the effects of abortion on subsequent reproduction, published in 1982 and sponsored in part by the U.S. government's Centers for Disease Control, found no evidence that abortion increases the risk of sterility, complications of subsequent pregnancies, or infant morbidity or mortality. As for the risk to the woman, a study published in the July 9, 1982, Journal of the American Medical Association, found that "between 1972 and 1978, women were about seven times more likely to die from childbirth than from legal abortion." . . .

Women Are Dupes

I believe most of these people feel that a woman entering an abortion clinic is incapable of knowing her own mind. Follow that reasoning down the road a piece and you deny women jobs, futures, choices, lives of their own, because of those hormonal changes that cause an "inability to think."

As radical action is prone to do, antichoice extremism clarifies the meaning of the right-to-life movement. The attempt of the mainstream right-to-life movement to present itself as secular and democratic is undercut as it tacitly accepts the vicious bullying of women outside abortion clinics. Here the movement is shown for what it is—not an attempt to save life, but a determination to control women's lives.

3 VIEWPOINT

"There is no principle that I could conceive under which destroying [abortion clinics]. . . could be in itself immoral."

Abortion Clinic Bombings Are Justified

Frank Morriss

In the last few years, there has been a rash of violent attacks on abortion clinics throughout the United States. Firebombings, vandalism, and harassment of clinic patrons are the tactics that a few, scattered members of the anti-abortionist movement have employed in their fight against legalized abortion. In the following viewpoint, Frank Morriss believes that bombing abortion clinics is justified. He claims that if individuals are unable to tolerate the immorality of legal abortion any longer, they should not be condemned for destroying the clinics in which these abortions are performed. Frank Morriss is a contributing editor to *The Wanderer*, a conservative Catholic newspaper.

As you read, consider the following questions:

1. Why does the author believe that the destruction of private property is justified in the abortion clinic bombings?
2. Why does the author compare slavery to abortion?
3. Do you believe circumstances exist in which it is permissible to violate the law? What are they?

I fail to understand the reasoning of those, both conservatives and others, who condemn destructive force brought against abortion facilities as immoral. There are many arguments against such actions, but immorality surely is not one of them.

We surely would not hesitate to destroy property in order to save the innocent lives of those already born. Why should there be any difference in the case of those unborn? If we knew of a building where conspirators stored explosives they planned to use in terrorist attacks, and we could not appeal to law enforcement officials to seize or destroy it, is there any axiom of morality that would prevent us from doing so ourselves, keep us from blowing it up where it was stored?

The hero of A.J. Cronin's *The Citadel* . . . helped blow up a defective, poisonous sewer that the city authorities refused to repair. Is anyone prepared to call that action illegal? Is anyone prepared to say it would be immoral to blow up the camps in the Soviet Union where international terrorists are trained?

But, the argument goes, it is illegal. The answer is that no legitimate law can protect another illegality, particularly one as deadly and heinous as abortion. If we are going to have to obey all actions that statutes allow or forbid, then we can hardly oppose abortion itself. Positive law does not stand against the natural law.

I can understand that non-Catholics such as Jerry Falwell, untrained in the nuances of metaphysics and lacking expertise in the natural law and in jurisprudence, would consider any destruction of property illegal, and therefore any destructive force against abortion facilities to be an evil means to a good end. But what excuses Catholic spokesmen who apparently follow the same reasoning?

Rejection of Force

I suspect in some cases it is a surrender to the rationale of pacifism. In such cases there is the actual rejection of force as a means of either self-defense or defense of neighbor. This indeed is one of the sorrowful possibilities of the tide of pacifism that is sweeping the Church in the U.S., particularly in our schools. If we may not use force to defend ourselves and our country, then we must passively surrender to evil under every circumstance, and let it do its worst. I can only point out in this case that pacifism is an error and an evil itself.

Some Catholics, however, might be misapplying or misinterpreting one of the principles of defense—namely that force can only be brought in response to actual attack. As a general principle that applies because we cannot judge other than by actions. If we could act on suspicion or surmise, great harm might be done.

Thus we could not suspect that someone planned an assault and, anticipating it, bring force against him. But that does not mean that the attack must be in actual final progress before we can respond. We need not wait for the cocked gun, the brandished knife, the lifted cudgel. We can strike down those threatening our lives or the lives of others as they move to the attack, or as they gather the deadly instruments, or sit in conspiracy issuing instructions. Of course the abortion attack has long been underway with deadly results.

John Trever, *The Albuquerque Journal*, reprinted with permission.

An attack once begun may be intermittent, but we need give the attacker no immunity during the periods of quiet. To do so would be to ignore the reason for defense and its purpose, and to grant to the attacker an advantage his evil intent allows.

Evil Facilities

Abortion clinics, even when not in use, are evil facilities containing the deadly instruments—the *situs* of the crime and the conspiracy. They are essential to a continuing attack on the innocent, just as were the concentration camps and gas ovens of the Nazis. There is no principle that I could conceive under which destroying them or putting them out of action for a period of time could be in itself immoral.

I say nothing about the practicality or prudence of such actions. I do not recommend them.

But neither do I believe we can consider them unthinkable, nor that we should shun or abandon those who have chosen that path. Surely there is a line that must be drawn beyond which we can no longer tolerate the continuation of abortion without whatever response to it is necessary to end it. If others have drawn the line at this moment of history, I am not going to be the one to say they have overreacted.

It is the standard reaction to ridicule the idea that God might tell someone to take destructive action against abortion. But surely God by His natural law and the rights and principles of that law tells us that there are evils that must be ended, and that it becomes a mere excuse when we say that we can only end them by the legal channels provided by the very system that has "legalized" the evil itself.

Slavery and Abortion

There came a time when slavery could no longer be tolerated while legislators and judges and officials failed to prohibit it. But slavery is in some ways a lesser evil than abortion—for its victims could say that while there was life there was hope. The marked victims of abortion face an extermination of hope almost at their beginning, along with their life.

It is more and more apparent that the time of toleration cannot be extended much longer.

4 VIEWPOINT

"Private individuals who oppose abortion do not have . . . sufficient reason to act beyond the civil law, at least in a violent way."

Abortion Clinic Bombings Are Not Justified

Robert L. Houbeck Jr.

Robert L. Houbeck Jr. is a librarian at the University of Michigan, where he is also working on a doctorate in European history. In the following viewpoint, Mr. Houbeck opposes clinic bombings because he believes legal channels have not been exhausted and that violence detracts from the just cause of the anti-abortionists' movement.

As you read, consider the following questions:

1. Why does the author criticize pro-abortionists' condemnation of the clinic bombers?
2. What are the circumstances in which the author believes that violating the law becomes a heroic act?
3. Why does the author believe bombing abortion clinics cannot be justified?

Robert L. Houbeck Jr., "The Clinic Bombings: On Pouncing and Prudence," *Catholicism in Crisis*, April 1985. Reprinted with permission.

One of the choicer ironies to have surfaced. . .in the abortion debate is this: Only the pro-life party, and not the pro-abortionists or their fellow-travelers, can explain why it's wrong to blow up abortion clinics. The pro-abortionists can't explain why it's wrong because they can't explain why anything is wrong. They have intellectually disarmed.

Pro-abortionists, you see, claim that one cannot distinguish between right and wrong for anyone but oneself. Abortion, as they explain it, may not be right for you, but you cannot legitimately make that judgment for anyone else. A wily Minnesotan has taken that moral reasoning seriously and in a few lines, deftly filleted that silly position: "Personally, I'm opposed to the bombing of abortion clinics, but I don't want to impose my morality on anyone else." How can pro-abortionists, given their brazenly asserted "Personally, I'm opposed" principle, justify imposing *their* moral judgments on other citizens who disagree with them and happened to express that disagreement in dynamite. Or aren't pro-abortionists serious about being "pro-choice"?

Solutions by Violence

Exquisitely futile, too, is the pro-abortionist complaint that violence against clinics should be deplored because it is, well, violent. Pro-abortionists are *nonpareil* practitioners of "solution by violence." That is, after all, what an abortion is: a solution by violence. The conceptus, they tell us, is not a person; it is property. Should this particular kind of property become a problem, the solution is, variously, to scald, slice up or pull him (or her) apart. Nor are these "solutions" as comparatively rare as the two-dozen odd other attacks on property that so worry the defenders of abortion. Rather, their bloody "sad necessities" occur at the rate of 3 per minute, 1.5 million per year. How, one wonders, can the pro-abortionists seriously object when other citizens, also sadly no doubt, resolve to "solve" this problem of mass abortion by a similar resort to violence against property? Aren't clinic bombings simply an uncomfortable application of their own principle of solution by violence?

The pro-abortionists, of course, faced now with opponents who reason as defectively as they, have been scurrying behind the law. Relativists in morals, they become positivists in practice. What is permissible, they hold, is whatever the law permits. As a placard at one of their rallies declared: "Abortion is legal; terrorism is not." If patriotism is the last refuge of the scroundrel, his first refuge must surely be the law. The law, the pro-abortionists insist, must be obeyed.

Yet these are the same folks who warn of the carnage that will ensue should abortion once again be proscribed. Women, we are admonished, will break the law and at their peril procure abortions anyway. How, though, if right is determined by the positive law—that is, by humanly constructed rules—how will these lawbreakers differ from the lawbreakers who today are tossing incendiaries? Both, however sincere, violate the civil law. Yet surely no pro-abortionist would suggest that a woman who would secure an illegal abortion was acting immorally.

Law and Abortion

The pro-abortionists, of course, are merely selective relativists and positivists. They do believe in absolutes. They absolutely want what *they* want. To hell with consistency: What they want is the right to abortion. Their problem is that they can't explain why anyone *ought* in justice to recognize that right. If tomorrow two or three personally opposed Justices really became personally opposed and joined with colleagues like Rehnquist and O'Connor in overturning *Roe v. Wade*, how many advocates of abortion on demand would believe that abortion, suddenly illegal, had also suddenly become immoral?

Ironically, only the pro-life party can explain why the bombings of abortion clinics ought to stop.

Many Legal, Legitimate Methods

There are many legitimate, legal methods anti-abortionists can use to try to sway public opinion. They can take a positive approach by providing counseling services for young, pregnant women who may be tempted to choose abortion because they aren't aware of alternatives.

They can lobby for a change in the law. They can hold marches and peaceful protests. They can distribute literature and speak out through the media.

But no one has the right to resort to terrorism in an attempt to force change. That's an irrational means of making an otherwise rational point.

Those who oppose abortion have the right to protest its legality. But they also have the obligation not to cross the line between free speech and harassment—and the line between peaceful protest and outright terrorism.

USA Today, November 23, 1984.

Pro-lifers insist on the distinction between the civil law and the moral law. The civil law is only law to the extent that it conforms to or at least does not violate the moral law. This moral law is not, as with the pro-abortionists, merely a matter of private sentiment or public statute; rather, the moral law is the natural law, which is the law of the Creator reflected in His creation. Man does not make this law, he discovers it. He discovers it, in discussion and debate with his fellows, by reflecting on what he is and what he was made for. Pro-lifers will concede that, as a matter of prudence, not everything that violates the moral law ought also to be illegal. The civil law, though, may not attempt to permit or to protect actions that grievously violate basic human rights of persons. To the extent that civil laws permit or protect grievous violations of natural rights of persons, those civil laws are unjust laws and *must* be opposed. Opposition to them, though, can take a variety of forms. Can one of those forms be the bombing of abortion clinics?

Pro-lifers insist that the bombing of abortion clinics is indeed wrong, but not wrong in the same sense that abortion is wrong. Abortion is an attack on the natural right to life of identifiable human individuals. Like rape or child molestation, abortion is intrinsically wrong, wrong because of what it is. No circumstance could ever make it right. Thus no civil law may ever permit it or protect it. Such a civil law, in fact, is no law precisely because law derives its authority solely from its conformity to the natural law, not from its being proclaimed in the proper way by the proper "authorities."

Similarly, laws which protect facilities that attack basic human goods, such as life, are no laws. To violate such unjust laws is not intrinsically wrong; rather, it is what such laws permit or protect that is intrinsically wrong. But the violation of unjust civil laws can be prudentially wrong, that is, wrong according to circumstances.

Attacking Laws Can Be Heroic

Violence against abortion clinics is prudentially wrong. To oppose evil, or, as [Thomas] Aquinas graphically phrased it, to "pounce upon" it, can be an act of heroism. Such pouncing, though, can also be an act of stupidity. It depends upon the circumstances, and the circumstances of 1985 America counsel against violence in the struggle for justice for the unborn.

First, private individuals who oppose abortion do not have, in today's circumstances, sufficient reason to act beyond the civil law, at least in a violent way. Blowing up an abortion clinic is not like blowing up a train carrying cyanide pellets to Auschwitz. Yes, abortion clinics are the places where doctors coldly slice up innocent human beings. But we do not live in a totalitarian society where all or even most political and moral recourse against this evil has been exhausted. In fact, the case is quite the opposite. . . . The tide may well be turning. What was permitted von Stauffenberg and his colleagues [who fought the Nazis] in their desperate situation is not permitted to us.

Second, clinic bombers, however well-meaning they may be, contribute to the dissolution of the moral community by helping perpetuate the delusion that whenever private individuals disagree with a law they become automatically empowered to disobey that law. What should be the exception becomes increasingly the norm. Civil order is a fragile construct. Any resort to violence against even unjust civil laws represents a grave decision. It is the sort, of course, that ought only to be followed by individuals capable of nuanced moral reasoning, after serious deliberation and after all other means of redress have been tried and exhausted. We must take care to be as concerned with preserving our constitutional order and our traditions of moderation and decency—the concrete guarantors of our human rights—as we are with overturning unjust laws. How we achieve our ends is as important as what we achieve.

Repelled by Violence

Finally, the American people, that majority we must seek to convince, are repelled by extremism. They instinctively—and rightly—reject the notion that 1985 America, for all its manifest wickedness, is like 1944 Germany. Any pro-lifer who becomes an apologist for violence against property risks muddling the real issue for these folks. Americans are a people of wholesome sentiments but sometimes blurry reasoning. Despite the powerful sanction of the positive law, they are coming to see. . . that those two-month-old "blobs of tissue" have arms and legs and suck their thumbs and are not blobs of tissue but are precisely what noisy pro-lifers have been insisting for years—unborn babies. Pro-lifers ought not to do anything that would obscure for that growing majority who the violent ones in this debate really are.

VIEWPOINT 5

"Those seeking to destroy Planned Parenthood clinics are seeking to rid the nation of what they believe to be slaughterhouses. They feel that justice is being denied to the innocent."

The Abortion Clinic Bombers Are Righteous Vigilantes

Aaron Everett

Aaron Everett is chairman of the Department of Modern Foreign Languages at Gustavus Adolphus College in St. Peter, Minnesota. In the following viewpoint, which is written in response to a letter the author received from Planned Parenthood, written by Katharine Hepburn, Mr. Everett argues that the abortion clinic bombers are linked to the tradition of old west vigilantism. Legalized abortion is inhumane, he maintains, and while the public should not wholeheartedly endorse the bombers, the cause that they espouse is a just one.

As you read, consider the following questions:

1. How is legalized abortion like terrorism, according to the author?
2. Why does the author believe that abortion is "cheating"?
3. Even though the author defends the abortion clinic bombers, he still does not support their actions. Why?

Aaron Everett, "When the Laws Do Not Protect," *The Wanderer*, March 28, 1985. Reprinted with permission.

In early February [1985] I received in the mail a letter with Katharine Hepburn's letterhead. Ms. Hepburn (I admire her immensely as an actress) began:

Dear Friend,

I am deeply troubled by a rising tide of vandalism, death threats, and other acts of terrorism now sweeping our nation—all directed at family planning clinics, their workers, and volunteers.

Fifty years ago my mother also spoke out for reproductive rights. She helped Margaret Sanger found an organization dedicated to providing birth control information for women in need.

. . .Terrorism in any form is not to be tolerated. We need your help at Planned Parenthood!

Ensuring Justice

I think it is safe to say that most of us are against terrorism but I think we must be careful about misusing words. Is Hepburn comparing the attacks on Planned Parenthood clinics to the attacks on the American compound in Beirut, Lebanon? There the purpose was to take lives. I believe that the purpose of those attacking the clinics is to save lives. I do not condone their actions but I do understand their frustration and anger.

First, let me say that I do not believe those attacking the clinics are terrorists. I believe they are vigilantes. It's an old American custom born in the Old West. Vigilantes are individuals who take the law into their own hands when they perceive that justice is not being done. We . . . saw an individual [Bernhard Goetz] who was attacked in the New York subway respond by shooting the four who intended to rob him. The public loudly approved the action. . . . On the news, there was a report of a senior citizen who, when attacked, set down his groceries, got out his revolver and shot those who were attacking him. It is almost a foregone conclusion that he will be roundly approved. People have had enough of not being protected by the "law." As the legal system fails to ensure justice and, as people discover that others approve of one's defending one's rights and those of others, we can expect vigilantism to spread like wildfire. Those seeking to destroy the Planned Parenthood clinics are seeking to rid the nation of what they believe to be slaughterhouses. They feel that justice is being denied to the innocent. Since it is the Supreme Court which has denied them the protection of the law, no help can be expected from the legal system. Therefore they feel compelled to take the law into their own hands to ensure justice.

In her letter, Ms. Hepburn declared: ". . . Terrorism in any form is not to be tolerated." Those attacking the clinics obviously agree.

They believe that the abortionists, with the approval of the Justices, are practicing terrorism. They oppose the activities of the clinics and their protection of "reproductive rights." The meanest things are done in the name of freedom and then given such nice-sounding names. To respond: "It's the law of the land!" is pointless. So was slavery and the denial of suffrage for women. The Supreme Court may declare abortion legal but those attacking the clinics believe they are struggling to uphold the right interpretation of the Constitution. For them, legalized abortion itself is terrorism. When the Supreme Court itself is the protector of terrorists, what is one to do?

Haven't we all said, of the Germans in Hitler's time, "Why didn't somebody do something?" Something like bombing the concentration camps? The Germans said they did not really know what was going on. That cannot be our excuse. We know and we approve gladly or permit it by our silence and inaction. . . .

Destroying Property Justified

Some have argued that destruction of private property to save the unborn baby's life is not justified because there are other legal recourses available. This is an incorrect argument not at all applicable to the plight of a particular day's abortion victims. Apart from sidewalk counseling the legal recourses available to us to stop the murders will have, at present, little chance of saving those babies who are currently scheduled to be executed at a particular time. It can be argued that in some cases there remains only one reasonable way left to those who are concerned with the 20 or so babies who are in imminent danger tomorrow at any given murderatorium, and that is by somehow carefully damaging the equipment which the operator uses to murder babies for money. One must ask himself how many babies one is willing to suffer to die in order to ensure the imagined benefits of that "law" which says private property is, in some cases, a more important good than innocent human life.

Hal Barton, *The Wanderer*, May 16, 1985.

There is a dreadful shallowness, a frightening levity about people who have no standard but the legal one. Then God is, indeed, dead, as the philosopher, Nietzsche, proclaimed, and then "all is permissible." Nothing worthy occupies the attention of such a society. It has lost its soul, bartered it for a few moments of selfish indulgence. It has no reason to survive and is moving mindlessly toward suicide. It is much later than we think. If we are blown up by a nuclear bomb, it will doubtless be set off by someone looking for the ultimate thrill.

I would not join those who are seeking to destroy the abortion mills. I do feel compelled to speak at every opportunity against squandering human lives. Unfortunately, too many protest: "Personally, I'm against it but I don't want to impose my morality on others." These people mean well. They wish to be considered as thoughtful and broad-minded when they say that. What they say, however, is simply nonsense. What would be the response of those individuals if someone said: "Personally, I'm against cheating but I don't want to impose my morality on others?" I'm certain they would instantly object and rightly so. Nobody hesitates for a minute to impose his or her morality in such a case. Each can see what he or she loses. Each recognizes that we have to have all kinds of laws and rules aimed at controlling and penalizing cheating. It is only common sense that, in order to survive, a society must condemn and punish cheating. If cheating goes unchecked and unpunished, the result is eventually chaos and the destruction of society. *It is only common sense that the morality of the sane must be imposed.*

Abortion Is Cheating

Honest reflection will show that abortion, too, is cheating. *Abortion is cheating on a monstrous scale.* We all do lose every time an abortion is carried out. God only knows how much we lose every time an innocent life is snuffed out for expediency and-or whim. The sane (majority or minority) must seek to impose its morality for the common good or else we shall surely be destroyed if we do not destroy ourselves first.

We must not sanction the activities of the arsonists and bombers but we must also recognize that their cause is just. The cause is just but the means are unacceptable. It should be clear to those who cry out against this destruction of property that for those attacking the clinics something much greater is involved here: the willful destruction of human lives. Until that is recognized and some corrective action is taken the opposition will and must continue. What those opposed to abortion must do is follow the example of the civil rights activists: picket abortion clinics whenever they are open for business. It may take longer but, in the end, some rights are not denied in seeking to assure other rights.

6 VIEWPOINT

"A small band of fanatics have set out to impose their political will through fear rather than persuasion."

The Abortion Clinic Bombers Are Fanatical Terrorists

Ellen Goodman

Those who support abortion, as well as those who oppose it, believe that the abortion clinic bombings are terroristic and unjustified. The following viewpoint is by national columnist Ellen Goodman. In it, Ms. Goodman argues that the bombers are cowardly fanatics. Because they have failed to gain support for their position through legal channels, they must attempt unjustifiable violence.

As you read, consider the following questions:

1. Why does the author believe the abortion clinic bombings are on the rise?
2. According to the author, how has terrorism affected the number of abortions being performed?
3. What does the author believe the government should do about the bombings?

Ellen Goodman, "Terror at Abortion Clinics: a Portrait of Fanaticism," *Los Angeles Times*, November 30, 1984.

The entries in the daily log are almost routine now. A bomb threat in Washington, D.C. Two more in Maryland. Another in Pennsylvania. A catsup-covered long-bladed knife found against a door in South Dakota.

Nothing extraordinary. No devices have gone off this week. Nobody has been hurt. You might even say that things have settled down since November 19, [1984] when an abortion clinic and a family-planning clinic, both in Maryland, were bombed. Certainly there has been no event as freakish as the one in Alabama on November 15, when a part-time abortion counselor, who had been harassed by anti-abortionists, arrived home and found her cat decapitated.

But Barbara Radford, the head of the National Abortion Federation that keeps track of these acts, has no illusions that the worst is over. Quite the contrary. "We've seen a rise in bombings, a rise in arson, a rise in death threats to clinic personnel," she said. [In 1984] alone 24 centers in seven states have been damaged by fire or explosion and so has her office. In addition, there have been 150 reported cases of vandalism and harassment.

There is no proof that pro-life groups are behind these incidents, nor do we know for sure that these acts are connected. But we do know that the bombings, the fires, the crimes are occurring in an atmosphere of general frustration, of escalating anger and mounting pressure for action among anti-abortion activists.

Pro-Lifers Take Direct Action

These groups have not won a legislative or legal battle in a long time. A constitutional amendment to ban abortions is stalled. The U.S. Supreme Court last spring reaffirmed abortion rights. Thwarted in one direction, some right-to-lifers have been shifting in another direction: toward direct action against clinics, patients and doctors. As Alice Wolfson of the Committee to Defend Reproductive Rights has said, "If they can't make abortion illegal, they're going to try to make it impossible."

Inside the pro-life movement, moderate leaders are losing ground to extremists. Once, a man like Joe Scheidler, the head of the Chicago-based Pro-Life Action Group, was scorned by the mainstream. While the moderates work to change the law, Scheidler specializes in harassing patients, disrupting clinics, invading with "truth squads."

Scheidler calls the moderate leaders the "wimpish pro-lifers," "the lily pads for life." Yet this year he was welcomed not only at the annual convention of the National Right to Life Committee but also in the White House. He joined other anti-abortion leaders when they met with President Reagan.

As the center has shifted, the radical fringe has moved further into more dangerous territory. The acceptance of aggressive tactics by moderates makes it easier for the bombers and burners to flourish. The radical ground is fertilized with rationalizations.

Scheidler, for example, says that "we intend to shut down the (abortion) industry." Of the bombers and burners he merely reports, "I don't condemn them, I don't promote them. What we've seen is some damaged real estate. . . . It's like bombing Dachau and getting away without hurting anyone." So, in turn, a criminal like Curt Beseda, convicted of four felonies against clinics in Washington state, uses this same reasoning to justify his acts: "Tomorrow no child will be put to death there."

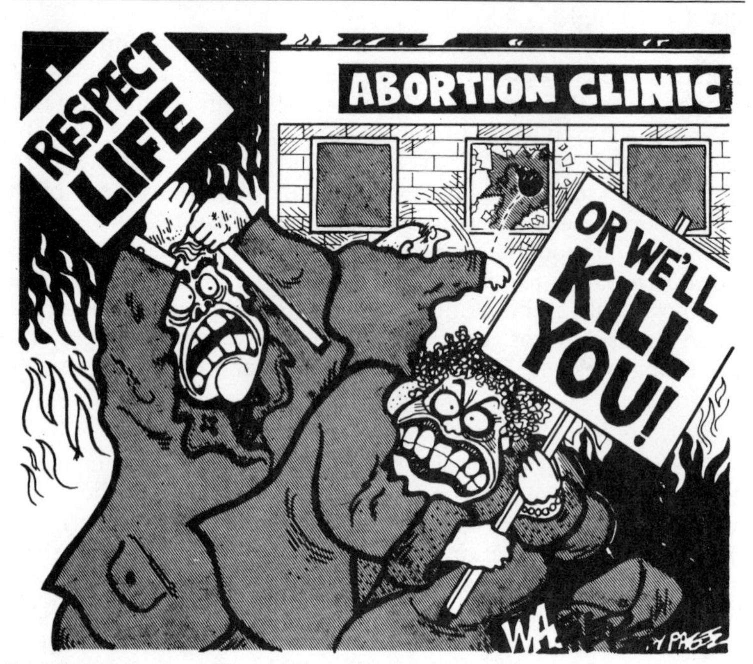

Pete Wagner, *City Pages*, Minneapolis, Reprinted with permission.

The tactics of "direct action" have escalated into a form of domestic terrorism. A small band of fanatics have set out to impose their political will through fear rather than persuasion. Those who cannot change the law by peaceful means justify violence. The most bizarre among them are even risking murder out of the conviction that they are stopping murder.

Women Cannot Be Harassed into Maternity

This terrorism has had no measurable effect on the number of abortions being performed. Women are rarely scared or harassed into maternity; we know that from years of illegal abortions.

But it does offer a close-up, a portrait of fanaticism at work in our culture. Fanaticism wears the same face whether it's in Lebanon or Maryland. Sometimes it even carries the same weapons.

President Reagan once described terrorists this way: "They are possessed by a fanatical intensity that individuals in a civilized society can only barely comprehend." This week his Administration launched its program to "get tough" on international terrorism. But we're still waiting for the condemnation of domestic terrorism that has taken place right down the street from the White House.

a critical thinking skill

Is the Use of Violence Ever Justified?

Abortion clinic bombings are condemned by both pro-life and pro-choice activists as being extreme and terroristic. A few anti-abortionists, however, believe that the harm that such acts prevent justifies the violent action. While almost all of us have at sometime wished to take the law into our own hands, especially when some other person hurts us, a friend, or a member of our family, we rarely do. Yet throughout history, in fiction, and in many of today's television shows, violent, illegal acts are depicted as justified if they further the cause of truth and justice. Do you think violence is always wrong or do you think some circumstances justify its use? This activity will give you an opportunity to think through your position on the use of violence.

Consider the four criteria listed below, taken from an article by Charles E. Rice in *The Wanderer*, a conservative Roman Catholic newspaper. Mr. Rice claims that the following four conditions must exist before an act of violence is justified.

1. To prevent a greater harm.
2. The harm to be prevented is immediate.
3. A direct relationship can be found between the action taken and the harm to be prevented.
4. No third and legal alternative is available.

Consider carefully each of the acts of violence described below. *Mark J for each situation you think would justify a violent response. Mark U for each situation in which a violent response would be unjustified.* In making your decisions use either the criteria described above or a rationale of your choice.

If you are doing this activity as a member of a class or group, compare your decisions with those of other class or group members. Be able to explain your answers. You may discover that others will come to different conclusions than you. Listening to the reasons others present for their answers may give you valuable insights into the causes and consequences of violence.

If you are reading this book alone, ask others if they agree with your decisions. You will find this interaction very valuable.

____ A military officer shoots a terrorist who has hijacked an airliner, has killed several passengers, and has threatened to kill more unless his demands are met.

____ A military officer shoots a terrorist who has hijacked an airliner and is threatening to kill all the passengers unless his demands are met.

____ A group of peace activists bomb a defense plant in order to protest the government's defense policy.

____ A group of anti-abortion activists bomb an abortion clinic after hours while the building is empty and the possibility of injuring clinic personnel or others is very slight.

____ A woman is being assaulted outside your bedroom window at midnight by a very large, threatening man. The woman is shouting, "Help me, help me." You take out a gun and shoot him.

____ A woman is being assaulted outside your bedroom window at midnight. From their conversation, you can tell they are man and wife. The woman is shouting, "Help me, help me." You take out a gun and shoot him.

____ An air squadron bombs the headquarters of a World War II concentration camp to free its victims.

____ You get in a drunken brawl with someone you dislike. This person starts shouting obscenities about your mother. You take out a gun and shoot him.

____ Someone murders a member of your family. The murderer is let off on a technicality. You decide to hunt her down and take justice into your own hands, murdering her the same way she murdered your family member.

____ While riding on a subway, you are accosted by four 17-year-old men carrying screwdrivers. They obliquely ask you for "change." You think they will stab you if you don't hand over all your money. Since you are carrying a handgun, you shoot them, but don't kill them.

____ A youth gang in your neighborhood is terrorizing local shopkeepers. You and a group of your friends challenge the youth gang to a fight.

____ Your high school team just lost a game because the other team cheated. You and your friends ambush the cheaters after the game.

Periodical Bibliography

The following list of periodical articles deals with the subject matter of this chapter.

Bryan Abas	"Right to Life or Right to Lie," *The Progressive*, June 24, 1985.
Christianity Today	"Violence Against Abortion Clinics Escalates Despite the Opposition of Prolife Leaders," February 1, 1985.
Dudley Clendinen	"Abortion Clinic Bombings Have Caused Disruption for Many," *The New York Times*, February 6, 1985.
Virginia Evers	"Real Babies and Phantom Bombs," *Conservative Digest*, October 1983.
Anne Finger	"Vigils Protect Clinics from Violence—for Now," *Guardian*, February 6, 1985.
Warren M. Hern	"The Antiabortion Vigilantes," *The New York Times*, December 21, 1984.
Albert J. Menendez	"The Flames of Fanaticism," *Church & State*, February 1985.
Rosalind Petchesky	"Bombing Feminism," *The Nation*, February 2, 1985.
Charles E. Rice	"Abortuary Bombing and the Justification Defense," *The Wanderer*, June 27, 1985. Available from 201 Ohio St., St. Paul, MN 55101.
William Schneider	"Terrorists and the Issue of Abortion," *Los Angeles Times*, January 4, 1985.
Joseph Sobran	"New Law, New Order," *Human Life Review*, Summer 1985. Available from 150 E. Thirty-fifth St., New York, NY 10016.
Cal Thomas	"Bombing Abortion Clinics: It's Violent, but Why Not?" *Los Angeles Times*, November 27, 1984.
Tim Unsworth	"Advice to Pro-Lifers: Treasure Life After Birth as Well as Before," *National Catholic Reporter*, December 23, 1983.
Ann Wharton	"Supreme Court Asked to Reconsider Abortion," *Moral Majority Report*, November 1985. Available from 305 Sixth St., Lynchburg, VA 24504.

Organizations to Contact

The editors have compiled the following list of organizations which are concerned with the issues debated in this book. All of them have publications or information available for interested readers. The descriptions are derived from materials provided by the organizations themselves.

Alternatives to Abortion International (AAI)
46 N. Broadway
Yonkers, NY 10701
(914) 423-8580

AAI believes women should not have abortions. The organization offers emotional, medical, legal and social support to women in problem pregnancies. It publishes *Heartbeat* magazine.

American Association of Pro Life Obstetricians and Gynecologists
266 Pine Avenue
Lauderdale-by-the-Sea, FL 33308
(305) 772-1853

The Association's members are obstetricians and gynecologists who do not perform abortions. It researches the adverse effects of abortion on women and publishes four newsletters per year.

American Association of Pro Life Pediatricians
2160 S. First Avenue
Maywood, IL 60153
(312) 531-3334

This anti-abortion association educates its members on the negative aspects of issues such as abortion and infanticide. Publications include a quarterly *Newsletter* and a book called *This Curette for Hire.*

American Civil Liberties Union (ACLU)
132 W. Forty-third Street
New York, NY 10036
(212) 944-9800

The ACLU champions the rights set forth in the Declaration of Independence and the Constitution. Among other activities, it works for safe and legal abortions for all women. The ACLU publishes a monthly newsletter, *First Principles,* a bimonthly newspaper, *Civil Liberties,* and a manual, *The Rights of Women.*

American Life Lobby
c/o America's Family Center
Rt. #6, Box 162-F
Stafford, VA 22554
(703) 659-4171

The Lobby's primary goal is a constitutional Human Life Amendment which would recognize the "personhood" of the unborn. It educates the public, monitors legalizations that concern abortion or infanticide, and maintains a library of pro-life material. It publishes a monthly newsletter, *A.L.L. About Issues*, books, booklets and information packets.

Americans Against Abortion (AAA)
6728 E. Thirteenth Street
Tulsa, OK 74112
(918) 836-2206

AAA supports adoption rather than abortion. Its publications include a monthly *Hotline* and "Thou Shalt Not Kill. . . My Babies."

Americans United for Life (AUL)
343 S. Dearborn Street
Chicago, IL 60604
(312) 786-9494

AUL promotes anti-abortion legislation to protect unborn human life. The organization runs a library and legal resource center. Publications include a quarterly newsletter, *Lex Vitae*, and a monthly newsletter.

Birthright, USA
686 N. Broad Street
Woodbury, NJ 08096
(609) 848-1819

Birthright, USA is a national volunteer organization dedicated to providing alternatives to abortion for pregnant women. The organization publishes *The Life-Guardian* bimonthly newsletter and various books.

Catholics for a Free Choice (CFFC)
2008 Seventeenth Street NW
Washington, DC 20009
(202) 638-1706

CFFC supports the right to legalized abortion. The organization educates Catholic women about abortion and contraception. It publishes *Conscience*, a bimonthly newsletter.

Catholics United for Life (CUL)
c/o Dennis Musk
New Hope, KY 40052
(502) 325-3061

CUL offers a Catholic perspective on family life and the value of human life. The organization advocates alternatives to abortion. It publishes a newsletter every six weeks and a quarterly *Youth Crusaders News*, as well as several books.

Choice
125 S. Ninth Street, Suite 603
Philadelphia, PA 19107
(215) 592-0550 [Hotline]

Choice supports the rights of women to make their own reproductive decisions. It educates the public about reproductive health care and offers quality medical service. It publishes a paperback for adolescents on reproductive health care called *Changes*, a guide to women's health rights in Pennsylvania, and books on parents talking to children about options in childbirth.

Forlife
PO Drawer 1279
Tryon, NC 28782
(704) 859-5392

Forlife disseminates a wide variety of pro-life material. These include films, filmstrips, plays, puppet shows, stories, books, monographs, pamphlets, and cassettes.

Friends of Family Planning (FFP)
122 Maryland Avenue NE
Washington, DC 20002
(202) 543-7803

FFP is primarily a political action organization. It opposes constitutional amendments or bills that would prohibit abortions.

Human Life Center (HLC)
St. John's University
Collegeville, MN 56321
(612) 363-3313

HLC, sponsored by St. John's University, promotes Catholic teaching on the sanctity of life. It publishes a teen pamphlet series and two quarterlies, *Human Life Issues* and *International Review of Natural Family Planning.*

National Abortion Federation
900 Pennsylvania Avenue SE
Washington, DC 20003
(202) 546-9060

The Federation is committed to making safe, legal abortions accessible to all women. It unites and provides information to hospitals, clinics, feminist health centers, etc., that offer abortion services and it instructs women on how to choose an abortion facility. Publications include *Guidelines on How to Choose an Abortion Facility* and *Minors and Abortion*, as well as a bimonthly bulletin and a quarterly.

National Abortion Rights Action League (NARAL)
1424 K Street NW
Washington, DC 20005
(202) 347-7774

NARAL is one of the largest membership and lobbying organizations working solely to keep abortion a safe, legal, and available alternative to all Americans who choose it. It works with the legislature, with the public and on college campuses. It publishes three newsletters per year.

National Organization for Women (NOW)
1401 New York Avenue NW, Suite 800
Washington, DC 20005
(202) 347-2279

NOW, the largest women's rights organization in the the US, supports safe and legal abortions and effective birth control. It is involved in political action and educating the public.

National Right to Life Committee
419 Seventh Street NW, Suite 402
Washington, DC 20004
(202) 626-8800

The Committee is a large organization that opposes abortion and euthanasia. It participates in political struggle against legalized abortion. Publications include the *National Right to Life News*, a biweekly, and *Challenge to Be Pro-Life*, a pamphlet.

Planned Parenthood Federation of America, Inc.
810 Seventh Avenue
New York, NY 10019
(212) 541-7800

Planned Parenthood offers women effective means of contraception, abortion and sterilization, regardless of income. It offers family planning services throughout the country and publishes books and pamphlets.

Pro-Life Action League
6369 N. Le Mai Avenue
Chicago, IL 60646
(312) 792-1997

The League intends to outlaw all abortion through a constitutional amendment. To achieve this goal it conducts demonstrations and picketing and is involved in lobbying. It publishes bulletins and brochures as well as an *Action News* monthly and *99 Ways to Stop Abortion.*

Religious Coalition for Abortion Rights
100 Maryland Avenue NE, Suite 307
Washington, DC 20002
(202) 543-7032

This Coalition of religious groups supports the right to make decisions about abortion based on conscience. It publishes a quarterly newsletter, *Options*, a Legislative Fact Sheet, and pamphlets and booklets.

Sex Information and Education Council of the US (SIECUS)
80 Fifth Avenue, Suite 801
New York, NY 10011
(212) 929-2300

SIECUS is one of the largest national clearinghouses for information on sexuality. The Council reviews books on human sexuality and compiles annotated bibliographies of sex education resources. They also publish a newsletter, *SIECUS Report*, and books, including *Winning the Battle for Sex Education, Adolescent Pregnancy and Parenthood, Media and Sexuality/Sex Education, Prostitution,* and *Oh No! What Do I Do Now?* They also have sex education curricula for all levels of students.

US Coalition for Life
PO Box 315
Export, PA 15632
(412) 327-7379

The Coalition sets up research programs in local pro-life, anti-abortion organizations, hospitals and government and health agencies. It publishes a *Pro-Life Legislative Services* monthly bulletin and a *Pro-Life Reporter* quarterly.

Value of Life Committee
637 Cambridge Street
Brighton, MA 02135
(617) 787-4400

The Committee fosters respect for human life. Its library includes a newspaper file on life issues.

Voters for Choice
2000 P Street NW
Washington, DC 20036
(202) 659-2550

Voters for Choice supports candidates who support pro-choice. It publishes *Winning With Choice*, a campaign strategy handbook.

Women Exploited by Abortion (WEBA)
1553 Twenty-fourth Street
Des Moines, IA 50311
(515) 255-0552

WEBA offers emotional support to women who regret having had abortions and counsels women considering abortion. It educates society about adverse effects of abortion. It publishes the pamphlets *Before You Make the Decision* and *Joy Comes in the Morning*, and the booklet *Surviving Abortion*.

Annotated Book Bibliography

Dave Andrusko

To Rescue the Future: The Pro-Life Movement in the 1980s. Toronto, Ontario: Life Cycle Books, 1983. Collection of pro-life essays covering a number of topics including morality, legality, and alternatives to abortion.

Rita Arditti, Renate Duelli Klein, and Shelley Minden, eds.

Test-Tube Women: What Future for Motherhood? Boston, MA: Pandora Press, 1984. Examines state-of-the-art reproductive technologies—sex selection, test-tube fertilization, surrogate mothering—and questions whether or not they are helping or harming women. Argues that women should dispense with doctors and learn the technology of abortion in order to perform it amongst themselves.

Edward Batchelor Jr., ed.

Abortion: The Moral Issues. New York, NY: The Pilgrim Press, 1982. Rather scholarly collection of classic viewpoints on the abortion issue with an anti-abortion bias.

Beryl Lieff Benderly

Thinking About Abortion. New York, NY: The Dial Press, 1984. Discusses the emotional, moral, social, and medical aspects of unwanted pregnancy. While the book emphasizes the practical issues of abortion—methods, emotional reactions—it concludes that abortion may be the only way some young women can come to terms with their fertility.

James Tunstead Burtchaell

Rachel Weeping: The Case Against Abortion. New York, NY: Harper & Row, 1984. The author covers a number of abortion issues to conclude that abortion is unjustified in any circumstances.

Edward F. Dolan Jr.

Matters of Life and Death. New York, NY: Franklin Watts, 1982. Impartial examination of the moral, religious, medical, and legal aspects of abortion, euthanasia, and in vitro fertilization. Gives pros and cons.

Paula Ervin — *Women Exploited: The Other Victims of Abortion*. Huntington, IN: Our Sunday Visitor, Inc. 1985. Comprised largely of personal testimonies of women who had abortions and who suffered from emotional, physical, and spiritual side-effects.

Fred M. Frohock — *Abortion: A Case Study in Law and Morals*. Westport, CT : Glenwood Press, 1983. Combines theoretical discussion with interviews with people on both sides of the abortion issue. Summarizes the legal, political, and personal aspects of abortion.

Jay L. Garfield and Patricia Hennessey — *Abortion: Moral and Legal Perspectives*. Amherst, MA: University of Massachusetts Press, 1985. Contains a wide range of perspectives on issues related to ethics and the law.

Germaine Greer — *Sex and Destiny: The Politics of Human Fertility*. New York, NY: Harper & Row, 1984. Covers a wide range of sex-related issues with a feminist slant. Promotes abortion as a form of safe birth control.

Beverly Wildung Harrison — *Our Right to Choose: Toward a New Ethic of Abortion*. Boston, MA: Beacon Press, 1983. Examines western culture's attitudes toward women, medicine, religion and law. Establishes abortion as a sound moral right.

Randall J. Hekman — *Justice for the Unborn: Why We Have Legal Abortion and How We Can Stop It*. Ann Arbor, MI: Servant Books, 1984. A judge details his experiences in denying teenagers abortions. Argues that the days of legalized abortion on demand are numbered.

Jeffrey Hensley, ed. — *The Zero People*. Ann Arbor, MI: Servant Books, 1983. A variety of prominent contributors argue against abortion, infanticide, and euthanasia.

D. Gareth Jones — *Brave New People: Ethical Issues at the Commencement of Life*. Downers Grove, IL: Inter-Varsity Press, 1984. Explores advances in medical technology and details the ethical dilemmas they present.

Peter Kreeft	*The Unaborted Socrates*. Downers Grove, IL: Inter-Varsity Press, 1984. The author brings Socrates back to life to examine the basic premises of the pro-abortion position. By engaging in a dialogue with an abortionist, an ethicist, and a psychologist, Socrates finds each of their arguments indefensible.
Kristin Luker	*Abortion and the Politics of Motherhood*. Berkeley, CA: University of California Press, 1984. Draws data from twenty years of public documents, newspaper accounts, and interviews with both pro-life and pro-choice activists. Promotes the idea that moral positions on abortion are tied to views on sexual behavior and family life.
Kathleen McDonnell	*Not an Easy Answer: A Feminist Re-Examines Abortion*. Boston, MA: South End Press, 1984. A feminist acknowledges the tendency to oversimplify the abortion debate. Concludes that while abortion should remain a woman's personal choice, the moral implications of the dilemma should be acknowledged.
Andrew H. Merton	*Enemies of Choice: The Right to Life Movement and Its Threat to Abortion*. Boston, MA: Beacon Press, 1981. Recounts grisly tactics of the pro-life movement. Concludes that the pro-life movement is hypocritical and dangerous.
Barbara Milbauer	*The Law Giveth: Legal Aspects of the Abortion Controversy*. New York, NY: Antheneum, 1983. Traces the history of the present controversy from its beginnings in the previous century. The author reports conversations with congressmen, doctors, lawyers, and others on both sides of the issue, but concludes that abortion is an essential constitutional right.
Bernard N. Nathanson	*The Abortion Papers: Inside the Abortion Mentality*. New York, NY: Frederick Fell Publishers, 1983. Discusses how the new science of fetology is responsible for proving the fetus is fully human. Also examines the pro-choice bias of the media.

Bernard N. Nathanson and Richard N. Ostling — *Aborting America.* Garden City, NY: Doubleday and Company, 1979. One of the best-known pro-life books. A former abortionist details his reasons for becoming anti-abortion.

Ronald Reagan — *Abortion and the Conscience of the Nation.* Nashville, TN: Thomas Nelson Publishers, 1984. Condemnation of the Supreme Court's decision to make abortion legal.

Joseph M. Scheidler — *Closed: 99 Ways to Stop Abortion.* Chicago, IL: Regnery Books, 1985. Suggests practical ways to stop abortion.

Arthur B. Shostak — *Men and Abortion: Lessons, Losses, and Love.* New York, NY: Praeger Publishers, 1984. Results of a survey of 1,000 men on the issue of abortion. The authors encourage men to participate in the the abortion decision and urge women and abortion clinic staffers to make this possible.

J.C. Wilke — *Abortion: Questions and Answers.* Cincinnati, OH: Hayes Publishing Co., 1985. Pro-life book in a question and answer format. Discusses prenatal development, fetal and newborn experimentation, the human life bill, and physical complications of abortion.

Index